To A[...],
God Bless,

View From a Bouncy Castle

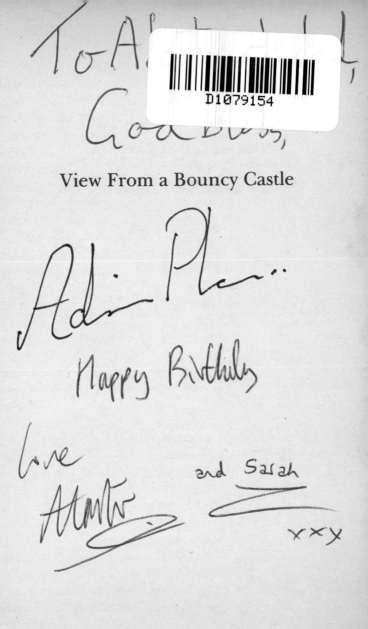

Adrian Plass

Happy Birthday

love
Alastair   and Sarah

xxx

View from a
Bouncy Castle

Adrian Plass

Fount
An Imprint of **HarperCollins***Publishers*

First published in Great Britain in 1991 by Fount Paperbacks

Fount Paperbacks is an imprint of
HarperCollinsReligious,
part of the HarperCollins Publishing Group
77-85 Fulham Palace Road, London W6 8JB

Printed and bound in Great Britain by HarperCollins Manufacturing, Glasgow

ISBN 0 00 627564-8

Contents

Bouncy Castle

You hear some funny things when you eavesdrop on your own thoughts. It happened to me the other day. I had been chatting to a very stolid, repressed sort of bloke, a nice chap but not easy to get close to. As I shook hands with him and said goodbye, I found myself thinking: 'You're a long way from the bouncy castle.'

It took me a while to focus on the origin of this homespun phrase or saying. But when I did track it down it was rather interesting.

A couple of years previously Bridget and I had been invited to the summer christening of Alex, the baby son of close friends of ours. The service went well, Alex was satisfactorily dunked

1

– to use a theological term – and the outdoor party afterwards was quite a grand affair.

There was lots of food, a lot of people, lots of sunshine and, in the middle of a grassy space at the back, a highly coloured, fully inflated, unpoliced bouncy castle.

Fed by a constant stream of stabilising air, it stood wobbling gently in the slight breeze, just waiting for small, excited children to clamber up and abandon themselves to bouncing, rolling, leaping ecstasy.

It didn't have to wait long, of course. The kids, hearing that the only rule was 'Take your shoes off!', were soon swarming all over it, relishing the fact that because it was hired 'without owner', there was very little in the way of restrictive supervision.

Nor was it long before the adults got in on the act as well. I was one of them.

I imagine that most parents will identify readily with my feelings about bouncy castles. We have four children, ranging in age from sixteen years old down to three and a bit (I shall be in trouble if I don't mention the 'bit'). In one and a half decades we have visited countless numbers of fêtes, fairs, school functions, agricultural shows and other open-air events, many of which featured the aforesaid attraction – but only for children!

Many a frustrated half-hour had I spent watching my offspring ricocheting wildly around on their inflated playground, while I smiled benignly, concealing my fierce inner desire to join

2

them. Always I was thwarted by the unrelenting presence of the proprietor, usually smoking one of those eternally dangling cigarettes, and occasionally coming out with professional phrases such as: 'Nobody over eight!' or 'This lot off – that lot on!'

The contrast between the dispassionate tone of these utterances and the tumbling joy of the kids used to depress me somewhat.

Now, for the first time, it was possible for fifteen years of frustration simply to disappear as I indulged my deep-felt need.

I have to confess that it took me a while to shake off my dignity and my shoes, but once I did it was wonderful. What the children thought about 18 stone of middle-aged man bouncing crazily from one side of their paradise to the other, I don't know. I wasn't too concerned at the time.

Most people got on during the afternoon, but there was one chap, Richard, who just couldn't seem to relax enough to have a go. He was one of those large, not very well co-ordinated men who look as if they were born in a suit. Now that he was grown up he wore it like a coffin. Very smart, very uptight, very dignified. At first he dismissed the whole idea of his using the bouncy castle as silly.

You could see him mentally picturing himself taking his heavy, well-shined black shoes off and leaping foolishly around like an inflated child.

But, as the afternoon wore on, I noticed that Richard was making gradual, unobtrusive moves in the direction of the castle. He would go and get another drink, for instance, then come back and stand just a little closer than before.

Every now and then his eyes would flick round and study the noisy bouncing mob with an odd mixture of fear and yearning.

Eventually, towards the end of the afternoon, he managed to stroll up to the castle apron, sit with tremendous nonchalance on the edge, and very casually remove his shoes, carefully unlacing them first. The jacket was next to go, folded neatly and placed on the ground beside him.

He then climbed carefully onto the castle itself and sat quietly at the side as though he was there in some sort of benevolent supervisory capacity.

He didn't sit for long. There is magic in the bouncy castle.

Before a minute or two had passed, that mass of congealed human dignity was flinging himself around wildly with the best of 'em, in a way he probably hadn't done for years. Down below, his large shoes stood neatly side by side in the middle of a jumble of other shoes. It occurred to me then how appropriate that was.

Rather like Moses at the burning bush, Richard had removed his shoes before treading the hallowed ground of joyful abandonment. For a short time he allowed himself to be a little child again and, as we all know, Jesus said that unless we become like little children we cannot enter the kingdom of heaven. I am quite sure that he did not intend this condition to be regarded as some kind of cold and arbitrary rule. Rather, he was saying that until we do acquire a child-like perspective we simply cannot see or understand the things of God, whether they be secular or specifically religious aspects of living.

The shedding of false dignity can be a very painful process (although the fear is often much worse than the fact – it was difficult to get Richard off once he'd got going) but every now and then, when we tread that hallowed ground for ourselves, we realise the wisdom of the Good Shepherd's words. Everything looks different from the vantage point of the bouncy castle. Get on with me now – there's no age limit – and we'll take a look.

Gardens
A Skip Full of Memories

I am not a keen gardener, to put it mildly. Every now and then, I dismally plod around our lawn behind the mower as it snarls and rips and chews at the grass like a toothless old lion. I might, if I am feeling more energetic than usual, do a bit of strimming as well. You know what strimmers are – those long things that buzz like demented insects, and drive you mad because you have to pull the nylon cord out a bit further every two minutes unless you've got the posh sort, which we haven't.

The only other thing I do in the garden is sit in it, usually just after I've finally got round to giving the lawn its short back and sides. I may not be very good at the practical side of things, but when it comes to occupying a garden chair with, say, a bottle of wine and half a cold chicken to keep me company, I am capable of displaying a concentration and single-minded persistence that would amaze many of those who think they know me. These latter talents have been very infrequently exercised however (a prophet in his own country, perhaps?) so, generally speaking, a little mowing, a spot of strimming, that's about the limit of my gardening activities.

My wife, on the other hand, is devoted to all growing things. A dedicated digger, planter-out and pruner, she has to be almost physically restrained from weeding the central reservations of motorways and the moss-filled grooves under the windows of other people's Morris 1000 Travellers. A real fanatic. She claims that if Paul Newman had proposed to her at the same time as I did, the deciding factor would have been the degree of horticultural commitment offered. An unlikely story, in my view, but there we are.

After a long early holiday a couple of years ago, my wife pointed out that the garden behind our house was beginning to acquire a sort of Matto Grosso quality. Would I do something about it? After a one-man safari into the undergrowth I went into the garage to look for a machete, or some other equally suitable tool. The garage was in a worse state than the garden. There might have been some tools there, but they were buried under about five years' worth of things-you-put-in-the-garage-because-you-can't-think-where-else-to-put-them. I realised that, before getting the garden done, we needed a skip.

It arrived after lunch, a huge metal bucket like a spare part for a tank. They delivered it, we would fill it up and they would collect it and dispose of our rubbish – at a price. It was lowered slowly outside the garage in a cloud of pink petals from our Japanese flowering cherry. I rolled my sleeves up and got started.

It sounds silly, but I got a bit emotional after a while. Some of the things I chucked into the skip were horribly concrete reminders of failed intentions, half-completed projects and even broken promises. Worst by far was the jumbled mass of wood, wheels and bits of wire that constituted my abortive attempt to construct a go-kart for my son Matthew when he was much younger. I remembered little Matthew waiting eagerly for it to be finished, and I remembered my own deep frustration as my ham-handed efforts resulted in complete and utter failure. My eyes were misting a little as I heaved this particular memory into the depths of the metal bucket. I've kept most of my other promises, and Matthew and I have a very good relationship now, but it was a painful moment.

As the afternoon wore on, the skip vultures descended. A friend who lives a little further down the road sauntered up and after some incidental conversation, mentioned that he had a fridge to dispose of. Would it be all right if he dumped it in my skip?

'Go on,' I said, 'shove it in!'

So he did.

Less than an hour later another friend who lived along the road the other way arrived with a little 'rubble problem'.

'Go on,' I said, 'bung it in!'

By the time a third supplicant had dumped his garbage in *my* skip, I was beginning to feel vaguely resentful. I try to be perfect but I'm not.

I wondered if a good night's sleep would produce a little more charity in me. It might have done but for the fact that on inspecting the skip the next morning, I discovered that some person or persons unknown had used the cover of darkness to deposit even greater quantities of refuse in my giant yellow dustbin. I hopped about furiously on the pavement in front of my house like one of those 'angry people' in a Charlie Chaplin film. I was seething.

'Why should they be allowed to put their blinking rubbish in my skip?' I muttered to myself when I had calmed down a little. 'Why should they? After all, I'm the one who has to pay for it in the end. Forty quid! It's not fair!'

'Big deal!' said the other end of a rather disturbing dialogue that occurs in my mind sometimes. 'You're paying forty pounds, are you? You may think that's an awful lot of money to spend on getting rid of other people's rubbish – '

'Yes, I do think exactly that!'

'Do you want to see a human skip?'

Then, in my mind's eye, I seemed to see a hill. And on the hill, nailed to a wooden cross, was a man in agony.

'Come on,' he called out, 'bring all your garbage up here, all your mistakes and failures and broken promises, all the things you can hardly bear to look at or think about, whatever they are and whatever you think about them; shove them on me – I'll get rid of them for you.'

'But who's going to pay?' I asked.

'I've already paid,' said the man. 'You go and get on with your gardening.'

The Gift of Weeding

I don't know how much Ascension Day means to most people. As a significant day in the church calendar it doesn't get much of a press, usually. Perhaps this is because it falls on a Thursday (nothing religious could possibly happen on a Thursday, could it?), and, let's face it, there are no chocolate eggs, pancakes, or gift-wrapped presents attached to its celebration. If we were a little more imaginative we might arrange to hire tall buildings for the day, so that Christians could make symbolic ascents in the lifts (or Vertical Personnel Distributors, as the Americans call them sometimes).

Ascension Day is, of course, the time when we remember Jesus' final farewell to his closest band of followers, the disciples. He had already, much more dramatically than Sinatra, made a number of comebacks, but now it really was 'goodbye' for the last time, and the Bible tells us that he was taken up and away from them in a cloud.

I saw a film once where they had obviously strapped a camera to the bottom of a helicopter for the Ascension scene. The disciples' hair was waving wildly in the wind from the rotor blades as the machine lifted.

I don't know how it happened in reality, but, however it was, he was gone, and that little collection of very ordinary people was left to wonder how on earth they were going to tackle the problems of the world without the power and charisma of his leadership. He had said something about sending a comforter to strengthen them but he had also warned that they would suffer more than he had, and he had made it very clear that the baton was being firmly passed to them.

It must have been a very thoughtful and somewhat worried little group of world-changers who drifted sadly away from the last, strange farewell.

And that is precisely how I feel when I try to pray for huge, impenetrable problems such as the situation in South Africa or the Middle East – thoughtful and somewhat worried, to put it mildly. How can I make any difference to the vast, complex set of difficulties that accompany political change in South Africa? Such a massive task: such – apparently – unresolvable issues. Surely my small prayer would drown in that sea of violence and prejudice and misery. It can seem a very dark world at times.

Fortunately, God does send us rays of light from time to time, and some of them, like little pocket torches, are re-usable. The one that helps me with this question of small prayers and big problems is a memory of something that happened to a friend of mine called Doreen.

Doreen and her husband, Geoff, are members of the house group that meets in our sitting-room each Thursday evening. We have become very fond of them over the years. Now at retirement age, they have qualities of cheerfulness, loyalty and ungrudging industry that are quite exceptional. One of the most reassuring sights that Bridget and I know is our two friends plonking themselves down on the big settee in our upstairs sitting-room every week at eight o'clock. They are good people.

One evening, Doreen arrived at the usual time for house-group clutching two big bottles of champagne, and with a great big grin stretched across her face. When the group had finally assembled, corks had been popped, and we each had a full glass, Doreen explained.

'Tonight', she said, 'we're celebrating the fact that I've weeded my neighbour's garden!'

Doreen had read the Bible passages in which Jesus says that we must love the people we don't like, as well as the people we do. Suddenly, as she read, she thought of the person who lived just down the road from her, a terribly bad-tempered old lady who talked endlessly when she wasn't being angry, and was popularly supposed to be very stingy.

Plucking up her courage, Doreen marched round to her irascible neighbour's house and offered to sort out her weed-ridden flowerbeds. The offer was received with predictable surprise, but quite unexpected enthusiasm.

'And it works!' said Doreen. 'It works! It really does! She's not bad-tempered at all when you get to know her. She's become so nice, and she's not stingy at all. She made me take some money for some plants I got her. Oh, and the lady up the road's doing a bit of gardening for her as well and – I don't know, there's so much love in it all!'

I know that the Gift of Weeding is not mentioned in Corinthians, but what a gift to have! There were tears in my eyes as I downed my champagne.

Doreen was celebrating her discovery that the Spirit of God still works in a suburban street in southern England in the nineteen eighties, and it inspired, and inspires me still, to believe that what could happen in a small way, could happen in a large way.

It is worth praying for South Africa. Every tiny defeat of prejudice that happens in that sad country as a result of the tiniest of our prayers, will justify the trust that, on Ascension Day, Jesus places in ordinary men and women using the power of his Spirit.

I don't know if drinking is allowed in Paradise, but, if it is, I would guess that, every time someone like Doreen lets love overcome hate and fear, the champagne corks must be popping all over heaven.

Trains
The Six-Forty to Charing Cross

Jesus once said: 'If your right eye causes you to sin, pluck it out and throw it away. And if your right hand causes you to sin, cut it off and throw it away.'

'It's better', he said, 'for an eye and a hand to be lost than for your whole body to end up in hell.'

Knowing what a lust human beings exhibit for the formation of new denominations and sects, it amazes me that we have not seen the development of groups of people whose members literally lop pieces off themselves and each other.

When I was going through my own very literal phase, the rather drastic approach to combatting sin that these verses suggested was very alarming, especially when I considered my own personal failings. If I had decided to remove the parts of my body that caused most problems, I would have ended up a decapitated eunuch — at least!

If, however, we agree and accept that Jesus did not intend us to interpret his words literally, what *did* he mean? I'm sure there are many shades of explanation, all quite valid. How about this one?

A friend of mine, whom I shall call Veronica, worked in a London office each week from Monday to Friday. Every morning she drove to the little country railway station near her home in time to catch the six-forty to Charing Cross. She didn't have to catch that particular train. The one that left at seven o'clock would have done just as well, but Veronica was one of those people who like to arrive early at their place of work, so that there's time to relax and take stock before launching into the business of the day.

The salary that Veronica earned was just what she and her husband Derek needed to keep their joint income at a reasonable level (Derek was a self-employed sculptor who worked from home). They were a very happily married couple in their mid-thirties, not just in love but also very good friends, an excellent advertisement for commitment.

The months passed and, in the course of her regular daily commuting, Veronica developed a nodding acquaintanceship with a fellow traveller — a man — who invariably boarded the same train as she did, but at the next station alone the line.

17

Gradually, almost imperceptibly, a friendship began and was deepened each morning during the hour-long trip to London. The man who sat on the opposite seat every day was civilised and charming, a very attractive person. Veronica was forced to face the fact that she had become that rare creature, a happy commuter. Her heart beat a little faster each time she boarded the train and found herself facing her new friend once again. She was on the verge of falling in love.

This is not, of course, a rare phenomenon in married people, and in many other cases might well have been an indication of neglect or thoughtlessness on the part of the husband, but Veronica and Derek really were very close, and they valued their relationship highly.

Veronica was troubled, and unsure what to do. After much thought she decided to ask for advice from her best friend – her husband. On the Saturday morning following that decision, she sat Derek down with a whisky and soda in the living-room and told him exactly what she was feeling.

Honesty compels me to admit that if I had been in Derek's position that morning I would almost certainly have produced some kind of ragged, emotional response. I used to tell myself that I was the civilised, level-headed type who could handle any crisis with deep, dark-brown-voiced calm. Experience has shown, however, that a small high-pitched hysteric usually takes over on these occasions.

Not so in Derek's case. He is a pipe-smoking, philosophical chap, the sort of man who enjoys pondering contentedly over a pint. He listened carefully to everything that Veronica said, sipping his drink occasionally and nodding in an understanding sort of way. Finally, she ran out of words and sat anxiously on the sofa waiting to hear what her husband would say.

There was a long pause, then Veronica spoke once more.

'I don't know what to do, Derek – tell me what to do.'

Slowly, deliberately, he rose to his feet, crossed to the sofa and sat down beside his wife. Placing his arm around her shoulders he spoke gently, but firmly:

'Darling – change trains.'

That was Derek's solution, and in this case it worked. If the six-forty to Charing Cross causes you to sin (don't cut it off exactly, British Rail will probably do that for you), go on the seven o'clock. Change trains.

Now, even I'm not naïve enough to believe that all or even most problems of this kind can be solved so simply. Even in Veronica's case, it cost her quite a lot to abandon the growing relationship that had brightened her mornings. It was worth it for her. For others there will be such complex considerations and so many difficulties, or perhaps things have gone so far that the 'changing trains' option is just not feasible.

But for people, Christian or otherwise, who want to avoid problems in the future, it is worth considering the proposition that it is easier to steer our lives and temperaments *round* obstacles, rather than meet them head-on, wrestle desperately with them, and probably lose the contest. Most of us know only too well the areas in which we are weak, or likely to be tempted. Often it takes a lot of courage and determination to change direction when sweet darkness is only a step away.

I know that Veronica's story doesn't sound much like the New Testament verses that I quoted, but it comes down to the same thing in the end, and the general principle holds good in all sorts of different situations. If you run into trouble, and it's not too late to do something about it, don't mess about – change trains.

The Four-Fifteen from Paddington

There was a time, not all that long ago, when I made sure that I never went anywhere, or did anything, that could possibly result in my looking foolish. As a result, you will not be surprised to hear, I rarely went out, and didn't do very much at all.

Far from producing humility in me, this limited approach to life made me into something of a clever-dick whenever I *did* do anything that was remotely useful. I have been coaxed, pummelled and persuaded into a much more vulnerable state over the past few years, but the clever-dickness (what an elegant expression!) is still part of me, and still has to be squashed by God from time to time.

One of the most memorable of these 'squashings' happened at London's Paddington Station when I was attempting to catch a train to the West Country – the four-fifteen to Taunton, as far as I can remember.

A very large number of people were queuing on the station concourse that afternoon, all keen to find seats on the fast inter-city train that was already being cleaned in preparation for departure.

I was as keen as everyone else. I wanted a seat in the second-class carriage adjacent to the buffet, so that I only had a short journey to fetch my coffee, sandwiches and – as a special treat on this particular day, I'd decided – a danish pastry. So intent was I on achieving this objective that I was prepared to sprint, suitcase notwithstanding, in competition with my fellow travellers, to make sure I got what I wanted. If there had been any starting blocks available I would have been crouched and ready for the gun.

Frustratingly, there were three false calls over the public address system as I waited near the front of the line of passengers. Three times a voice announced: 'The four-fifteen is now ready to board', and three times the same voice announced: 'We apologise for an incorrect call. The four-fifteen to Taunton is not yet prepared for boarding. Passengers are requested to return to the station concourse until further notice.'

Goodness knows what was going on behind the scenes. I never did find out what caused this rather excessive break-down in British Rail communications, but there was no doubt about its effect on the people in the queue. They – or rather, we – were muttering and fretting and tutting with impatience and irritation against the common, corporate enemy.

Then, just as I was preparing myself for the fourth attempt, the other end of that same disturbing (but familiar) dialogue, began to speak in my mind.

'Why are you racing against all these people?'

Feebly, I replied, 'Because, er . . . I want a seat next to the buffet so that I can get sandwiches and er . . ."

My reply trailed off pathetically.

'You're in the wrong race!' said the other end of the dialogue, and again – 'You're in the wrong race.'

As I turned these words over in my mind, I realised that the O.E.O.T.D. was absolutely right. I had become so taken up with writing books and making broadcasts and speaking to groups of people, that I was beginning to lose touch with the roots of all this activity, namely, my relationship with Jesus and my responsibility to God.

'Right! Okay! Good lesson, God,' I said brightly to the now clearly identified O.E.O.T.D., 'Buffet time now, eh?'

But to my horror, the same voice now said, 'I want you to walk round to the end of this queue of people, then, when the time comes, stroll down to the train, and I will save you a seat in the carriage next to the buffet.'

Full of faith, I said, 'No chance!' After all, I reflected, creating the universe was one thing, saving a seat on the four-fifteen to Taunton was something else. Obviously, God had never travelled by this train before . . .'.

Besides, I'd always found this business about 'God saves parking spaces for me when I ask him' extremely difficult to accept. Now, typically, I was being artfully manoeuvred into testing out a very similar principle. I decided that I'd better do what I was told.

Moving round to the back of the queue, I felt very foolish. When the fourth call to board came through the loudspeakers and I started my slow-motion amble towards the train, I just felt annoyance.

'I know what happens now, God', I said. 'I get to the train and there's no seat for me, and I'm expected to say "Hallelujah" anyway! and oh . . . I've been here before!'

The rest of the passengers were doing precisely what I'd known they would do. They were heading, as one man, for the buffet region of the train. I was heading for it too – very slowly, every muscle tensed with the effort of not running. When I boarded the carriage at last it was exactly as I'd expected, packed solid with people sitting and standing. There was just one vacant seat, right at the end of the carriage, immediately next to the buffet.

I stood beside the empty seat for some time, waiting for its rightful occupant to return from wherever he or she had gone. Eventually, when nobody claimed it, I spoke to the girl in the neighbouring seat.

'Is anybody sitting here?'

'No,' she said, 'it's free.'

So I sat down.

'I told you so!' said the other end of the dialogue. There is no smugness in the divine nature of course, but the O.E.O.T.D. did sound rather satisfied with itself.

Once again my clever-dickness was squashed, but I never really mind when these things happen. There is such wit and wisdom in the workings of the Holy Spirit. He is never dull.

I should add that my experience on Paddington Station is not an indicator that God will invariably reserve seats for his followers whenever they use public transport. I wish he would! It would make my life much easier. Rather, it was further evidence of the way in which God uses living parables to teach his children, and a reassuring reminder that those parables are engineered with individuals in mind.

Children
A Bedtime Story

It is possible to find hope in the most desperate situations sometimes.

The subject of homeless children in London and other big cities seems to come up frequently in news and documentary programmes nowadays. These are youngsters who have quite literally run away from difficult home situations, or from County Council homes for children in the care of the local authority. Some of them are frighteningly young. Not much imagination is needed to picture the kinds of pitfall awaiting naïve twelve- or thirteen-year-olds who are homeless and penniless in the big city environment.

These references always attract my attention because until I changed course a few years ago, my working life had been spent with children in trouble. I hesitate to describe them as 'disturbed' children, as an awful lot of my charges were – potentially – quite normal kids who had been struggling desperately to survive among highly disturbed and inadequate adults. They had, as Jesus puts it in the parable of the sower, no root in them – none of the good soil that is produced by consistent care and warmth and discipline and approval. I would be the last to deny that each person is responsible for his or her own actions, whatever the effect of background and circumstances, but there was a bleak inevitability about the downward progress of the fortunes of some of those children that was heartbreaking.

In the late seventies I spent eighteen months working in a secure assessment unit in the Midlands. This 'locked facility', as it was rather grimly called, existed to cater for children who were either too violent or too likely to abscond, to be placed in one of the open units that existed on the same campus. During their stay of a few weeks each child was assessed, and eventually despatched to a long-term placement of some kind.

Reasons for placement in this double-locked, seven-bedded little world were sometimes bizarre in the extreme. One boy, a harmless enough looking lad, was in the habit of collecting together stray dogs from the area around his home and setting them on little girls for 'fun'. I well remember my mother-in-law bravely visiting the unit and chatting to this particular boy for some time. Afterwards, totally unaware of his strange hobby, she said, 'I really can't think why he's in here. He seems a very normal sort of boy. We had a lovely chat about dogs – he's very interested in them, isn't he?'

Another boy, no more than twelve years old, was admitted to the unit after failing in his attempt to kill, by drowning, a little girl of six who had tormented him for a year by calling him 'Fatty' every time they met. His account of how he lay in wait for her, pushed her into a stream, then held her head under the water with his boot until she seemed to be dead, was chilling, to say the least.

Some of the older teenagers, seventeen- or eighteen-year-olds, were hard, unrepentant delinquents, who could never be fully trusted in that environment. There were never fewer than two staff members working with that little group of seven 'visitors', although the atmosphere could actually be very warm and pleasant at times, depending on which staff were working, and the particular mix of kids at the time.

I have such a jumble of memories of that place; moving, grotesque, depressing, all kinds, but one that always comes to mind when I look back at that year and a half is the memory of an incident that might contain a little bit of inbuilt hope for all of us.

It was an evening when an outsider had come into the unit by special arrangement to show the boys how fluffy toys could be quite easily made as presents for mothers or little sisters or girlfriends. Four of the toughest residents had opted for this activity, and were soon deeply absorbed in the sewing and sticking and stuffing of various toy animals. Having made it quite clear to me that their efforts were purely directed towards the happiness of those who would eventually receive the toys as presents, they worked with quite unprecedented care and concentration for the whole session. It was one of those nice, quiet evenings.

Later, when supper had been eaten, and the unit tidied up, each boy washed and went into his single bedroom for the night. It was then my dismal duty to go from room to room, locking the door of each one securely after a brief chat with the occupant. The four boys who had been involved in the toy-making happened to sleep in the same row of four rooms.

In the first one I found that Ben, a villainous and battered fifteen-year-old, had sat his newly assembled squirrel up in bed beside him, and was reading it a goodnight story. I closed the door quietly and moved to the next room.

Sammy, a dangerous and unpredictably violent lad, was just kissing his rabbit goodnight.

In the third room Peter, a genuinely charming fellow who seemed completely unable to refrain from running away and pinching things, was already fast asleep, a little woolly head on the pillow next to his.

In the fourth room was Brett. Brett was certainly not a sentimental type. The grinding difficulty of his early life and clashes with authority figures of various kinds ever since had convinced him that life was a dark and unfriendly jungle, a place where you simply couldn't afford to show any weaknesses at all.

Brett was lying back, staring at the ceiling. The squirrel he had made earlier was dropped carelessly onto the chair beside his bed.

'Your squirrel not going to bed with you then, Brett?' I asked seriously. 'He looks a bit lost lying on the chair there.'

'Don't be daft!' grunted Brett. 'I'm seventeen – I'm not a kid any more.'

'No,' I thought, as I locked the door, 'you haven't been allowed to be a kid for a very long time.'

Half an hour later, when I peered through the little square glass window in Brett's door, I saw two things. First, he was asleep. Secondly, there was a shoe-box on the floor next to the bed. Inside, tucked up cosily beneath tissue paper and a handkerchief, Brett's squirrel slept beside his maker.

What is hopeful about all this? It reminds me that in all the years I worked with children and young adults in trouble, I never met one whose inner child had been completely extinguished. However tough or hardened, there seems to be a part of every individual that could still, potentially at least, respond with the simplicity of a small child, and that is the part of us that God calls to himself, whether it is lost in a city or in a lifestyle.

'Suffer the little children to come unto me,' said Jesus, knowing that many of them are locked up inside people who have not been kids for a very long time.

Sportsday

My children asked me the other day what I enjoy watching most on television. After thinking about it for a bit I realised that the answer was sport in general, and athletics in particular. My special favourite is the relay. There's something about all that bursting energy and the giving of everything in a co-operative effort that really touches me. And it doesn't have to be the Olympics or anywhere near that sort of standard. Nor does it have to be on television of course; live events are always exciting.

It was exactly the same when we used to hold our own sports day at the boarding school for maladjusted boys where I worked many years ago.

What is a maladjusted boy? Well, basically he is someone who is unable to cope with, or adjust to, the situation he is living in, often through no fault of his own. In fact, it would be fair to say that in many cases known to me, the parents were far more maladjusted than their children, and only too happy to project their own unhappiness and disturbance onto a son who could be removed like an amputated limb and despatched to boarding school. Other boys came from homes where parents genuinely loved and cared for their children, but through grindingly negative circumstances had been unable to hold their families together as they would have wished.

The boys at this particular school all came from difficult backgrounds of one kind or another, and they were almost invariably more experienced at losing than winning. Consequently sportsday was a very tense and important occasion, especially as some of the participants would have parents coming along to watch.

We had some incredible characters taking part in these races. I remember one lad called Vincent, a very amiable kid, and the most incompetent criminal in the world. He always got caught, but never seemed to mind very much. He came out on a trip to Bristol in the school van once, together with a couple of the other boys, and cackled loudly and suggestively when we stopped to allow a pregnant girl across the road.

'I don't see what you're laughing about,' I said, 'all the people you can see around us are the products of pregnancy.'

'Oh, I know,' said Vincent, suddenly very earnest, 'I used to live in Bristol.'

Whether he believed that birth through pregnancy was a phenomenon peculiar to that city, or whether he was claiming to have fathered the entire population of Bristol, I was not absolutely sure.

Vincent had never won anything. Fifteen years of being an unwanted extra in his own home had left him with no genuine confidence at all. He had to act big.

Then there were kids like little Donald. Donald was a few years younger than Vincent, but, if anything, he'd probably had it even harder. His dad had knocked him about every day for years, and he'd ended up a bit like Piglet in Winnie the Pooh books, quivering with willingness to please, but very nervous, and sort of wispy to look at. Donald used to go out first thing in the morning to hug the trees, and he quite often wrote letters to himself. He wanted a real friend more than anything else in the world.

I found him once in the boys' telephone room trying to get a bewildered operator to put him through to his father. I tried to help for quite a long time until Donald happened to mention that there was no telephone in his dad's house. Even after I explained, he didn't really understand.

'The other boys phone their dads,' he said, 'why shouldn't I phone mine?'

I did my best to describe the telephone system in as painstaking a manner as possible, but he still remained unconvinced, and clearly thought that some kind of deliberate unfairness had been perpetrated on him. Secretly, I considered it a blessing that he had no easy access to the harsh and uncaring words that he would certainly have heard from his father if that kind of regular contact had been possible.

Donald would love to have won something in the school sports – anything really – preferably with his dad watching. For despite everything that had happened, his father was still the only person whose approval really counted.

It is a matter of record that neither Vincent nor Donald ever did actually win a race on sports day. Vincent was a very tall, skinny lad whose feet stuck out in the quarter past nine position. He ran like a penguin – not a born sprinter.

Donald was not exactly a natural athlete either. When he accelerated his legs seemed to be trying to escape from his body to left and right, while his trunk moved in an averagely straight line. I swear that his ears streamed in the wind like Piglet's when he picked up speed, though.

They never won – but they didn't half try! That's what used to bring the tears to my eyes, the desperate, red-faced, trying to win against all odds. I admired it then, and I admire it now.

There's an awful lot of talk in the Church nowadays about TRIUMPH and OVERCOMING and VICTORY, but that sort of talk often (not always, but far too often) comes from church leaders and speakers who have talents and ambitions and vested interests that leave the Vincents and Donalds of the Christian world puffing away hopelessly at the rear.

One of the things that infuriated people about Jesus was his refusal to enter the kind of political, social or religious races that they wanted him to win. He turned the accustomed social order upside down, too busy with the Vincents and Donalds, the so-called losers, to win other people's races for them.

He is the same now, and the words he used two thousand years ago are a promise for ever to those who try hard, but just can't manage to win.

'The first shall be last, and the last shall be first.'

Pistols at Dawn

Earlier this year our house group was divinely inspired (well, we were inspired to decide – oh, all right, it just seemed like a good idea) to study some of the parables. Parables might be broadly defined as stories that keep you entertained on the front door-step while the truth slips in through a side window, and Jesus was of course a master of the genre. There's always something new to be discovered in these expertly crafted little tales.

We opted to begin with the parable of the wheat and the tares which, for those who are interested, is recorded in the thirteenth chapter of Matthew's gospel. In it, we learn how a farmer's enemy secretly sows thistles among his wheat during the night, and how the farmer decides to let the thistles grow until harvest time, because uprooting them might harm the genuine crop. Later in the same chapter Jesus explains to the disciples that the wheat represents the children of the Kingdom, and the thistles are people belonging to Satan, sown by the Evil One to disrupt God's chosen ones.

Naturally, every member of our group is a dazzling example of total transfiguration, but I did wonder, as our discussion progressed along very satisfactorily interesting and stimulating lines, whether any of my fellow pilgrims had experienced, as I had, an involuntary spasm of self-doubt as they listened to the story.

'You're a tare! You're a tare!' screamed the loud voice of my old insecurity. 'Call yourself wheat, you weed? You must be joking!'

'Calm down,' said the quiet voice of kindness and reason. 'You may be a bit stunted and defective in the ear department, but you are wheat. You are *my* wheat. Understand?'

It's taken me a good many years to hear and trust that quiet voice. Goodness knows what I'd do without it nowadays, though.

I don't know if any of the other group members were actually wrestling with inner fears that they might be sons of the evil one, unconsciously planted to do damage to the saints, but I do know that a lot of Christians find it much easier to believe they are condemned than forgiven and wanted. I meet people all the time who have spent their lives feeling guilty about everything under the sun. They probably apologised at birth to their respective midwives for taking up so much valuable time. This particular vulnerability, the tendency to take on the 'Jonah' role in any and every situation, does not make life easy, to say the least.

When my oldest son, Matthew, was a little boy, he went to a small junior school in Norfolk. Mrs Shaw, the headmistress, was small in stature, but a mighty force in the little world that she ruled with awe-inspiring competence and total assurance. One day, Matthew, only just five years old, climbed down from the school van at half past three with a doom-laden expression on his normally cheerful little face. Half an hour and two tear-dampened jam sandwiches later, we knew what the problem was. He had been walking along in the playground that afternoon just before coming home, when he happened to put his hand in his pocket and discovered a coin left over from the weekend. Pulling it out too quickly he lost his grip on the ten pence piece and dropped it onto the tarmac. Immediately he was pounced upon by a representative of that awful race, the 'Big Girls'. She reminded him, probably with a great deal of relish, that Mrs Shaw had said some very cross things last week about children who brought money to school.

'You wait', said the big girl, 'till I tell Mrs Shaw you had some money. You'll be in trouble tomorrow.'

Matthew was petrified. In his mind Mrs Shaw made the Spanish Inquisition look like the Red Cross. Tomorrow was going to be the worst day of his life – and possibly the last. We were quite worried really. Matthew obviously thought that his headmistress was going to kill him. What should we do? After much thought I decided to write a letter to Mrs Shaw, in which I would challenge her to a duel. It was the only thing that sprang to mind. As far as I can recall, it began as follows:

Dear Mrs Shaw

Matthew is terrified that you might kill him in the morning because he accidentally brought money to school with him yesterday. I am therefore challenging you to a duel on the hill overlooking the school. I am happy to allow you the choice of swords or pistols. If you win, then you may punish Matthew's abominable crime in any way that you see fit. If I win, then he remains unpunished . . .

My only worry as I sealed the envelope was that she might accept my challenge. I'm quite sure she would have won.

The letter seemed to do the trick. The head-mistress wrote back to say how much she and the other teachers had enjoyed the letter, but she also commented on how it had made her realise that loud public condemnations aimed at real offend-ers, might sometimes bring terror to small, inno-cent people who hadn't quite understood. Mrs Shaw was really quite nice after all.

Some of the statements that Jesus made are very frightening. They were meant to be. He never pulled punches or compromised the truth when something hard needed to be said. But how tender and forgiving he was with individuals who were conscious of their sin. He still is, especially with worried wheat like you and me.

I'm quite sure that when Jesus was here on earth in his physical body, there must have been many small, nervous people who would have tugged the master's sleeve after one of those awesome speeches about hell-fire and gnashing of teeth.

'Err . . . excuse me,' they would have said, 'I don't think I'm going to make it.'

'Don't worry,' he might have replied through the side of his mouth. 'I'll see you later. It's that lot I'm after.'

And 'that lot' were the hypocrites, the phar-isees, those who claimed to be getting everything right, the ones who placed impossible burdens on the shoulders of those same small people, who wanted to be good but knew they weren't succeeding.

We do not pray for the rigid justice of Christ, the dislike of God and the unfriendliness of the Holy Spirit to be with all of us. Grace, love and fellowship are the attributes of God that warm us and draw us together. God hates all sin, a fact that he makes abundantly clear, and the law is the law. But when it comes to the crunch, he's almost as nice as Mrs Shaw.

Heads and Hearts

More than thirty-five years ago my grandmother died. For the whole of her married life and since the death of my grandfather, she had lived in a detached house called 'Cabinda' near the top of a hill in the little Sussex town of Heathfield. Next to my parents I loved Nanna more than anyone else in the whole world. She was the only person, for instance, other than Mum and Dad, who was allowed to see me with no clothes on. Travelling the fourteen miles by bus from Tunbridge Wells to visit her was always an enormously thrilling adventure, sometimes I thought my heart would burst with excitement and joy as my mother and I passed through the front gate and caught our first sight of the familiar thin figure waiting to greet us at the door.

When I think about her now a wave of images flood my memory. Her face was a bright light ringed with grey hair, and she always seemed to wear the same green cardigan. She had a spinning top that belonged to my mother when she was little, but still hummed as if it was new. There was a big cardboard box filled with a wonderful assortment of items to make things with, and a drawer full of blown birds' eggs, and a garden that rambled down to a pear orchard at the bottom, and stone hot-water bottles, and a Bible like a pirate's treasure chest with big brass clasps. Nanna always had plans for being nice to people that you could help with, and lots of time to read stories, and things to do in the kitchen that involved using funny old-fashioned tools and containers, and a scullery that was one step down from the kitchen, and a discarded pre-war car in the field beside the house that I used to sit in and pretend to steer. So many memories gathered in such a short space of time.

I was only six years old when Nanna died. It was the age of the stiff upper lip. 'We all have to be very brave,' my mother said, but I couldn't be at all brave when I heard the news. It was like a blow to the head, shocking and painful beyond belief. Almost immediately afterwards, though, a numbness replaced the pain. Somehow, unconsciously, I managed to hold the unwelcome piece of information in the back of my mind without letting it touch or affect my heart, the place where you really believe things.

Some time after Nanna's death I set out one morning to walk the fourteen miles from Tunbridge Wells to Heathfield. At the time I seemed to be motivated by a stubborn determination simply to visit the town that had always been so special in my life, but in retrospect, I am quite sure that I was actually setting out to prove to

41

myself that my grandmother was still alive, what-ever anyone said. Armed with fivepence worth of sweets I embarked on my journey. I told my parents where I was going, but, quite reasonably, they didn't take me at all seriously. Children of my age just didn't do things like that. They thought I was playing a game.

All through that day I trudged along the bus route that I knew so well from those countless trips to see Nanna, every now and then eating one of my little stock of sweets, and hoping that it wouldn't be much further.

Meanwhile, my frantic parents had contacted the police, who were searching the area around my home on the assumption that I was lost, or had been abducted from some local spot.

By five o'clock that afternoon, sweetless and weary, I had walked as far as Mayfield, nine miles south of Tunbridge Wells, and still five miles short of Heathfield. It was there that the truth hit me at last. Nanna was dead. There was no point in going on. If I reached Heathfield and walked up the hill, Cabinda would still be there, but it would be no use going through the front gate and knocking on the door because there was nobody to open it any more. Nanna was dead. I turned round and began the long journey back to Tunbridge Wells.

Much later I arrived home to be greeted with overwhelming relief from my parents and a telling-off from the police.

It hadn't been a wasted journey. The truth about my grandmother's death had now made the eighteen-inch journey from my head to my heart. Because of the particular way I was made I had needed my Mayfield walk for that to happen.

We are often painfully insensitive to this need in other people when they appear stubbornly unresponsive to our gospel-spreading endeavours. For many folk it is not just a matter of receiving information about the Christian faith. There often has to follow a journey – emotional, intellectual, spiritual, or all three – which allows that information to become a personal reality in their lives. Stomping around impatiently with size sixteen evangelical boots at this stage is unhelpful, to say the very least.

I am reminded, in this connection, of an incident involving my son David when he was about seven years old. We were on holiday in Wiltshire at the time and visiting a village not too far from Salisbury. As usual we drifted into the parish church and began that slow-motion perambulation peculiar to church explorers. After roaming around for several minutes I came to a small side-chapel. Inside I discovered David, standing with the stillness of deep concentration, in front of an old oil painting of the crucifixion. Peering over the top of my son's head I studied the picture that was so absorbing his attention.

It was not one of those idealised, rather unreal portrayals of Jesus on the cross. The artist had obviously set out to demonstrate the appalling physical suffering that this barbaric punishment inflicted on its victims. The Jesus in this picture was haggard with pain and exhaustion, flecked with blood from the wounds caused by a cruelly depicted crown of thorns, and sweating with malarial profuseness. It was a painting of someone who could only welcome death.

David has been hearing tales and talks and readings about Jesus since he was a baby; about his life, his teaching, his death and his resurrection. The facts about the crucifixion were certainly known to him, but the expression on his face as he turned around and spoke was an unfamiliar one. Shock and compassion filled his voice.

'They didn't half hurt Jesus, didn't they, Dad?'

The knowledge had entered his heart. They really did hurt Jesus, and he really did die on that cross.

But he really did come back to life as well.

Jesus is dead. Nanna is dead. But David and I expect to see both of them again one day.

What Katy Said

The best Easter present I ever had was my daughter Katy.

I must be honest and confess that, far from being planned, our fourth child was what one might term an 'after-not-thought'. Bridget and I already had three sons and we loved them very much, but we very definitely did not want another one. When Bridget discovered that she was pregnant in 1979 it was very hard for her or me to rejoice and be thankful. On the contrary, we felt weary and apprehensive about the prospect of adding yet another infant to our collection. We already felt disorganised enough with three.

Additionally, Bridget was at an age when health problems for mother or child could easily arise during pregnancy, so quite frankly, both of us were frightened and nervous about the whole thing.

As the nine months passed we gradually cranked our attitudes up onto a rather unstable level of optimism, talking with brittle brightness about the baby boy who was due to be born in March. Very rarely did we allow ourselves openly to consider the possibility that it might be a girl. Instead we shrugged, as people do, and said, 'Well, just as long as it's healthy we don't mind what it is'.

I can't speak for my wife, but as far as I was concerned, every repetition of that well-worn cliché was a twenty-four carat lie. I wanted a girl. Oh, how I wanted a girl! By the time that nine months was up, the heavenly in-trays must have been piled high with applications in triplicate, signed by me, and all saying the same thing: 'Let it be a girl!'

The birth took place at about four o'clock on March the ninth. It was hard work for Bridget, but there were no complications. At the moment when the midwife held our fourth child up to be inspected by its mother, Bridget was so geared up to joyful acceptance of a boy-child, that, despite the evidence of her eyes, she cried, 'Oh, the little darling, it's a boy!'

I have made some famous mistakes in my time, but not on this occasion.

'No, Bridget,' I said, checking once more with a quick glance, 'I'm pretty sure that's a girl. . . ."

The midwife agreed, and with a majority verdict against her, Bridget soon changed her opinion.

It was a girl. It was Katy. And what a gift she was. To the three boys, because she quickly became a focus for love and affection. They changed her, they looked after her, they cuddled her and they adored her. They were utterly entranced and captivated by her.

To Bridget, for most of the same reasons, and because having Katy meant that she was no longer stranded in a house full of males.

To me, because something brand new had come into my life. I was one of three brothers, one of them two years older than me, the other two years younger. I knew nothing about little girls and how they grow up. It was enormously exciting to have this small jewel of a person living in the same house as me, sharing my life and teaching me so much. As Katy's personality developed, so the things that she said and did began to suggest all sorts of other ideas and connections.

I recall, for instance, a train journey from Polegate to Brighton when Katy was still very much a baby. As the train approached a tunnel, just after leaving Lewes Station, she put her thumb into her mouth. Our carriage happened to hit the darkness at precisely the same moment. By the light of the sixty-watt bulbs that dully illuminated our carriage, Katy removed her thumb from her mouth and stared at it in amazement.

'Good heavens!' she was obviously thinking, 'all I have to do is stick this in my mouth and the daylight gets switched off!'

The train emerged from the tunnel and, full of expectancy, she popped her thumb in again. Nothing happened of course, but she was undismayed. All the way down to Brighton, and all the way back later on, she repeated the experiment with little loss of enthusiasm.

I couldn't help but reflect that many denominations are founded on less . . . .

Much more recently, in the year when Katy became three, I strolled into the garden one sparkling April morning, to find my diminutive daughter pushing one arm up as far as it would go towards the sky. In her outstretched hand was a single bluebell, newly picked from the border beside the lawn. As she offered her flower to the shining early sun, she identified it with loud ecstasy.

'DAFFODIL!!' she shouted, 'DAFFODI-I-IL!!'

I am as tediously obsessed with accuracy as most parents. I corrected her gently.

'No, darling' I said, 'it's a bluebell.'

Not one inch did she reduce the length of her stretching arm, not one decibel did she lower her volume: 'BLUEBELL!!' she shouted, 'BLUE–BE-E-ELL!!'

Katy's joy was in being part of the morning and having a beautiful flower, not in anything so trivial as being right. She accepted my pedantic correction, but it didn't change anything important.

If only those of us who are Christians were more like Katy in the garden, less concerned with how right we are in our individual emphases and dogmas than with the joy of being one with Jesus.

'YOU HAVE TO SPEAK IN TONGUES TO BE A CHRISTIAN!!' one of us might shout ecstatically.

'No, you don't', God might correct us gently.

'YOU DON'T HAVE TO SPEAK IN TONGUES TO BE A CHRISTIAN!!' we would shout with undiminished joy.

Not long before the incident in the garden I took Katy to a show performed in a nearby hall by a local amateur dramatic society. This year the special attraction for children was an afternoon performance of *The Wizard of Oz*. Katy was excited and a little bit scared. She knew the story well, and liked all the characters except one, the Wicked Witch of the West. This was the character who had sent her scurrying to safety behind an armchair when the story appeared on television in cartoon form. Like most children of her age, Katy was not yet able to separate fact from fantasy in some areas.

Now, as I dressed her in woollies, ready to walk down the road to this live presentation, she tried to reassure herself.

'Daddy,' she said solemnly, 'there won't be a Wicked Witch of the West this time, will there? Eh, daddy?'

'Well, I think there will be, darling,' I admitted, 'but why don't we think of something to say to her when she comes on, so that we won't be scared?'

Katy considered this suggestion seriously for a moment, her brows knitted in concentration. Then her face cleared, 'I know what we'll do,' she said brightly, 'why don't we just say "One – two – three – BOO!" when we see her, then we'll probably be all right, won't we?'

'Sounds good to me, Katy,' I replied, 'let's just practise a few times before we go.'

A little later, word perfect in our defensive ploy, we set off in the exciting darkness to walk to the hall, Katy still whispering 'One – two – three – BOO!' at intervals, just in case the witch might be hiding behind a garden hedge or in the branches of an overhanging tree.

The inside of the hall, when we arrived, was filled with light and noise, lots and lots of children laughing and chattering with their mums and dads. Such a cheerful atmosphere was it that Katy forgot all her earlier fears as she gossiped with acquaintances and contemporaries.

At last, the lights dimmed, the curtains opened, and the show began.

Katy loved it. She pointed everything out to me as if I was blind. There was the little girl called Dorothy, and there, a little later, was the scarecrow, then the tin man, and finally the lion (the 'nice' lion, as Katy hastened to point out). So far, so good, but eventually there came the inevitable moment when a green spotlight was switched on, and the wicked witch appeared, cackling horribly, her long bent nose almost touching her long, bent, wart-covered chin.

Amateur dramatic societies are not always able to produce convincing portrayals of benevolent or morally neutral characters, but when it comes to evil caricatures they really go to town. They did on this occasion. This witch was very unpleasant indeed.

Katy was terrified. Forgetting all about 'One – two – three – BOO!', she dived under my overcoat and pressed against my chest as if she was trying to get right inside my rib-cage. Nothing I could say or do would persuade her to come out until it was absolutely guaranteed that the witch would not reappear.

Later, after the show, she treated my explanation that the witch was just an ordinary lady dressed up with the scorn that it deserved. An ordinary lady is an ordinary lady – a witch is a witch. Silly Daddy!

I wondered, as we arrived home, if it had been a mistake to take Katy at all, but already, as her coat was being removed, she was telling her mum all about the entertainment with great animation. Clearly, the fear was a part of the whole experience, and probably wouldn't do her any harm.

Looking at my daughter a little later as she tucked into her fish-fingers and baked beans, I thought about the Wizard of Oz, and how the story closely reflects what I want for Katy, and what God has always wanted for each of us.

Like the scarecrow, I want her to have a brain that is creative and strong. I would like her to have a heart that is generous and loving, like the tin-man. And, of course, I hope she will be as brave as a lion, especially when the wicked witches of this world appear. I'm sure she'll find something more effective than 'One – two – three – BOO!' with which to defend herself.

Most of all, perhaps, I would like Katy to carry through life the same urgent and excited desire as Dorothy (and, incidentally, the prodigal son); and that is, quite simply, a yearning, in the end, to go home.

Coming Home
A Near-Fatal Encounter

If Jesus decided to pay an extra-curricular visit to claim the accrued royalties on his parables, more than one publisher would disappear in a cloud of holy smoke. Just about every Christian preacher in the world would have to shell out ten per cent of Caesar's own as well. For two thousand years now these sparkling little stories have been used to comment and illustrate and prove and disprove and reinforce and undermine and entertain in an endless variety of publications, pamphlets and sermons.

Take the Prodigal Son, for instance. I began to take a special interest in this character one autumn evening after I had been speaking at a college in Manchester. I was staying in what I can only describe as a grotty hotel room, deep in the heart of some nameless suburb. It was the sort of hotel where they chain the television to a water pipe fifteen feet up the wall so that it can't be easily pinched. It was only possible to see the screen properly by lying flat on my back on the bed, staring up towards the ceiling.

No doubt, on some deep level, I thanked God for my accommodation, but on a superficial and worldly plane I was absolutely cheesed off. Lying there in my rented tomb, almost breaking my neck in an attempt to watch some rubbishy TV programme, I started to have a very bad attack of good old-fashioned homesickness. One by one I pictured the members of my family – Bridget, Matthew, Joseph, David and Rosey the dog. A wave of misery engulfed me as I imagined them all moving and having their being in the warmly familiar surroundings of the house and town where we live.

For a time I ceased to be a complex human being. All that I was or had ever been was concentrated into one yearning desire. I just wanted to go home. I wanted to be in the place where I really belonged, where I slotted into a shape that was *my* shape, a perfect fit through constant use. And it was when that uniquely painful sensation was at its worst that I thought about the prodigal son, ragged among the pigs, suddenly feeling what I was feeling only much more so, and deciding it was time to go back.

The story is so well known now. That feckless lad has been leaving home loaded and light-headed, then returning broke and bowed, over and over again for twenty centuries. Every detail of his briefly-recorded history has been drawn out carefully with the theological tweezers and laid under the bright lights of exegetical study to be examined from all conceivable angles.

The story of his dramatic fall and rise (did you know that 'Prodigal Son' is an anagram of 'No-God spiral?') has brought comfort, repentance and simple understanding to millions of souls over the years, not least because of the eternally heartwarming picture of a God who picks up his skirts and runs with a passion much greater than forgiveness to embrace the miserable broken specimen that used to be his son.

There's no mistaking the joy with which he offers a cloak and a ring where a harsh word and a blow are expected. Then the dash back to the house, the bustle of a hastily-prepared party, and the famous fatted calf feast. An orgy of happiness and relief, too bright to be dulled by the Pharisaical elder son's moaning.

The whole tale is a stunning revelation of God's excited willingness to displace sin with love.

'So what?' you may ask. 'We knew that.' The thing is, lying in that Manchester hotel room, I began to feel rather puzzled. Why do so few church-going people seem to have experienced that joyful collision with God? What about the ring and the cloak and the fatted calf? How come lots of Christians I meet feel that God is graciously but rather distantly allowing them to hang around on the edge of the kingdom on sufferance, instead of showering them with affection and signs of his love?

It's as if God had taken the prodigal back, but treated him according to his self-valuation as a hired servant rather than a son. What goes wrong? Consider this . . . .

The Prodigal Son abandons his job with the pigs, just as in the parable, and sets off towards his father's house, nervous about his reception but determined to go anyway. Not long after the start of this journey he is intercepted on the road by an enthusiastic but deluded individual who has heard only a distorted account of the father's habit of forgiveness.

He doesn't quite believe in it, but he thinks he does, and he'll feel a lot happier when he's not alone.

'Hi!' he greets the trudging penitent. 'Good news – you've been forgiven!'

'Great!' says the prodigal.

'Here you are', says the deluded one, and he wraps an imaginary cloak around the lad's shoulders. He mimes the action of putting a ring on his finger. Together they sit down to eat a nonexistent fatted calf with invisible knives and forks.

'Isn't it wonderful!' he enthuses.

'Oh yes!' responds the prodigal, intensely relieved that he is to be forgiven so painlessly. 'Yes it is!'

They meet regularly for mime sessions. They become very proficient at mime. At last the young man manages to express a growing concern.

'The, er . . . cloak and the ring and the calf – they're not actually, er . . . real, are they?'

His lack of faith is rebuked and disciplined. He feels guilty and unhappy. He knows the things are not really there, and he doesn't actually feel forgiven. Where is the father?

Eventually he either settles for the troubled half-life of tediously repetitive mime sessions, or he goes back to the pigs; or, if he's got any sense, he leaves his mime instructor behind and moves on down the road to risk a genuine encounter with his father, who is anxiously awaiting him with a real cloak, and a real ring, and a real fatted calf.

And real forgiveness . . . .

Death by Atrophy

The 'mime' thrives where religious activities are atrophied and conducted only out of a sense of duty.

Jesus wasn't interested in captive audiences. He didn't need to be. The people heard him gladly. So gladly did they hear him that thousands of them forgot to make lunch arrangements on at least two occasions because they were so captivated by the things he said and the way he said them. It didn't matter about food. The loaves and the fishes turned up, and Jesus was very resourceful when it came to trivial essentials.

Is it foolish and shortsighted to ask why the Body of Christ on Earth — the Church — demonstrates so little of this natural drawing power nowadays? Why are so many Christian communities locked into the monotonous repetition of those 'mime' sessions that I mentioned in the last section? You do see a Christ-like attractiveness in some groups and individuals: famous ones like Billy Graham, and completely unknown ones like a little old lady who lives half a mile from me. People like this attract without bribe or coercion because the life of Christ has become an indistinguishable part of *their* lives. They glow unselfconsciously.

Perhaps that's the problem with our religious activities, that we allow the sacred and the secular to become unhealthily separate. Take Bible study and prayer groups for instance. Malcolm Muggeridge once said that the Church is man's way of keeping God at bay. An exaggeration perhaps, but well illustrated in many home-groups that I've experienced, where such exercises as Bible study, prayer and hymn/chorus singing actually act as walls to prevent the wind of the Spirit from blowing change and adventure in people's lives. And it happens in every kind of denominational setting, from very traditional to very modern.

My own denomination, the Church of England, is far from guiltless in this respect. Revival has come to many parts of the anglican world, but we are still prone to be rather stiff and resistant to necessary change.

There comes a point in the communion service, for instance, where, in many anglican churches, a strange tension creeps into the atmosphere, a tension compounded of fear and apprehension. A Martian or a Baptist would be very puzzled. What could possibly be causing the clammy palms, the nervous glances to left and right, the troubled shifting from foot to foot, the shallow breathing, the white-knuckled grip on the service book?

The answer, of course, is that the congregation is about to be encouraged to 'Exchange The Peace'. A friend of mine tells me that every muscle in her body tenses when this moment arrives. 'Well, I'm not hugging *him*,' she mutters to herself as she glances at her left-hand neighbour, 'and I'm certainly not kissing *her*! A couple of handshakes and a quick mumble and that's my lot – back to pretending to read the service book!' I realise that a great many people *do* enjoy the Peace, but an awful lot of others are still going through an unfreezing process. Habits die very hard in religious communities, including bad habits.

Have you, for example, ever been in the following kind of House Group or Bible study meeting?

Leader: (*Nervously*) Right – well I've got the vicar's/pastor's/elder's questions here, and we've just read the passage, so here goes. (*Reads from a sheet of paper.*) Do we think the leper was er, pleased or er, upset to be healed? (*Pause as everyone drops into the shampoo position to study their fifteen different versions of the Bible and find the answer to the question 'in the text'.*)

Doris: (*Uncertainly, with her finger keeping the place in her Bible*) Er . . . I think he was pleased.

Leader: (*Nodding impartially*) Hmm . . . interesting. Er . . . Richard – any thoughts?

(Pause)

Richard: (*Bent frowningly over the passage*) Er . . . I think he was *very* pleased.

Leader: (*Nods slowly for a few seconds as if turning over these responses in his mind*) Okay . . . right . . . well, I think we've probably gone about as far with that as we can go.

Such a meeting will then proceed to a bone-shatteringly tedious time of prayer, during which numerous half-hearted requests twitter uselessly against the brass heavens and flutter back to earth unanswered. Finally, there is only Mrs Bissington's elbow to be prayed for before the 'religious' part of the evening is properly concluded. At last, the elbow is duly interceded for by some public-spirited volunteer, the Grace is said with a sincerity fuelled mainly by relief, and all those present relax into the blessedly natural atmosphere of 'coffee and biscuits time'. If only some of the warmth and energy of this latter period could have crept into the 'God bit' earlier. Perhaps if the group had allowed their spiritual activities to grow out of relationship with God and each other, instead of vaguely assuming that such things were obligatory from week one, the quality of the whole meeting might have been quite different by now. An awful lot depends on leadership that is secure enough to explore, and wait, and build patiently, and see God's hand in *everything* that happens.

Deadly Dim-Dominant

Negative and atrophied leadership styles are by no means confined to the traditional denominations. In those churches where spontaneity is much more carefully organised, the incessant need to maintain an optimum spiritual blood temperature can result in some strange behaviour.

I have quoted elsewhere (and it is an entirely authentic quote) the worship leader who, carried away by his own enthusiasm, told his congregation that, after the next chorus, he wanted to hear a 'spontaneous round of applause'.

That kind of thoughtless comment arises, more often that not, from a fear that things are not 'buzzing' spiritually in the way that one might expect if God was really present in the service or meeting. Insecure leaders will occasionally project their fears onto those they are leading. I once knew a church elder who almost invariably stopped the service, usually in the middle of a chorus, to announce that he sensed a 'spirit of heaviness' in the room, that was preventing people from worshipping freely.

His confidence could only be restored by something blatantly spiritual happening, preferably accompanied by tears of grief, relief or repentance on the part of some co-operative individual. (Tears have always been rather popular in some sections of the Christian world, perhaps because the release of emotion in one person reduces the pressure on all the others.) I'm certainly not suggesting that the Holy Spirit doesn't or can't work in situations like that, but inciting others to produce spiritual-type behaviour as a means of reassuring ourselves is surely not terribly constructive.

I have already suggested that religious activities such as Bible study and prayer can actually keep God out of small group situations. This happens especially when such activities have not grown out of relationship, and where (particularly in the kind of church I've just been describing) the leader is unable or unwilling to allow genuine discussion.

Let me introduce you, for example, to a character called Mister Dim-Dominant, or DD for short.

DD has been selected to lead a housegroup mainly on the basis that he says the right things in the right sort of religious language.

In public his air of assurance is so great that some people slip into a miserable awareness of their own spiritual inadequacy for as long as they're in his orbit. Highly intelligent or well educated people are particularly vulnerable in this respect.

Somehow DD manages to convey that his shining persona is made possible by the light of the Spirit passing directly through a heart and mind unshadowed by the dark forms of knowledge and reasoning power.

'My knowledge', DD seems to be saying, 'is supernatural in origin. Lay down your flimsy, worldly tools of intellect and creativity, and I will instruct you.'

The truth about DD is that he is neither as naïve, nor as spiritual, as he appears. He has simply discovered a role which glosses over some yawning cracks in his faith, life and temperament.

In the meantime, rather unfortunately, he has been placed in a position of leadership and authority over a group of Christians who need more solid help than he is able to offer. DD's housegroup is not a happy affair. It usually consists of everyone sitting in a circle miserably telling each other how good God is, and how rotten they all are.

DD, with his crinkly smile and air of assurance, is like a small, one-bar electric fire at which the group members attempt to de-ice their frozen faith.

DD maintains his dominance through well-orchestrated discussion sessions. In the following example he has pinned a large rectangle of white paper to the wall by his chair, and a black marker-pen is poised in his hand.

DD: (*Nodding significantly and smiling insightfully at members of the group.*) Okay! Now, we're going to have a real old brainstorming session. I've got a question for us to think about, and I'll just stick the answers up on the wall here. Okay?

(*The group makes a noise like a herd of depressed cattle, indicating agreement.*)

DD: Okay, and here's the question. Who is Jesus?

(*Dismal silence*)

FRED: (*Meekly, knowing he's almost sure to be wrong.*) Er . . . He's the Messiah?

DD: (*Showing pastoral kindness to Fred.*) Yep! Okay! He's the Messiah . . . (*Writes* Messiah *in tiny letters at the edge of the paper*) . . . but, Who is Jesus?

(*Dismal silence*)

MARY: (*Not very hopefully.*) He's the Saviour.

DD: (*Writes* Saviour *in even tinier letters at the edge of the paper.*) Mmm . . . yes, he's the Saviour . . . (*in deep, meaningful, authoritative tones*) . . . but Who is Jesus?

(*Beams around with shining, questioning eyes.*)

BOB: (*Trying to hurry along the coffee and biscuits.*) Is he the mighty counsellor?

DD: (*Writes* mighty counsellor *in minute letters along the top edge of the paper.*)

63

Thanks Bob, he's the mighty counsellor, but . . . (*puts his bottom lip between his teeth in an expression of fatherly, playful chiding*) . . . come on folks – WHO IS JESUS?

BRENDA: (*Preset for failure.*) He's not the Son of God, is he?

DD: (*Delighted and thrilled.*) The Son of God! Jesus is the son of God! (*Writes* THE SON OF GOD *in huge letters that cover the paper on the wall.*) Jesus is the Son of God! What's Jesus . . .'?
(*DD conducts with his arms as the group recites the correct answer like a class of infants learning their tables.*)

GROUP: Jesus-is-the-Son-of-God.

DD: I think that's from the Lord!

In junior schools this is called 'focused questioning'. It is heavily discouraged by those who train teachers. Why is it all right in the Church?

Mister Dim-Dominant is not malicious, just misguided.

But when leadership of this kind is allowed to continue, a lot of people can get hurt and confused.

The example I've given portrays a caricature – but only just!

Breakage in the Pickle Aisle

Outsiders are unlikely to be attracted by church communities which are stuck in the 'mime' situation.

Some time ago I walked into a supermarket to buy a pound of sugar. It was one of those huge places where shoppers drift trance-like, with wild eyes, down the wide aisles as strange music softly plays. Ghastly – and fascinating.

As I set off to hunt down the sugar (supermarkets 'hide' the sugar for obvious commercial reasons) I noticed a huge sign hung above the tills. Its message was printed in large, vivid, red lettering This is what it said:

CROSSROADS VALUES CUSTOMER
CO-OPERATION. WE WOULD BE
WARMLY GRATEFUL IF SHOPPERS
COULD REPORT BREAKAGES OR
SPILLAGE IN THE AISLES. THANK
YOU!

I registered this information vaguely as I trailed dismally around the store searching for my humble purchase, but just after I discovered the sugar (tucked away between toilet rolls and garden compost) I remembered it with sudden clarity, for there, in front of me, lay a beauty of a breakage or spillage. A big fat jar of Piccalilli sauce, the yellow glutinous stuff with chunks of something-or-other in it, had fallen on to the floor where it had burst like a huge ripe fruit. The resultant mess, a yellow, glass-littered sludge, was quite spectacular.

'Time', I said to myself, 'for a bit of customer co-operation. Here's where I earn some of that warm gratitude.'

Clutching my pound of granulated, I made my way unerringly to the 'Twelve items or less' queue, anxious to report my discovery. Idly, I found myself counting the purchases in the basket held by the lady in front of me. 'One – two – three – four . . ." The discovery that she had thirteen items to pay for filled me with a quite irrational fury. For some reason, taking thirteen things through the 'Twelve items or less' exit seemed, at that moment, a much greater crime than murder or genocide.

I wanted to proclaim loudly to the whole world the depths to which human nature was capable of sinking. But I didn't. Instead, I contented myself with imagining the warm gratitude with which my co-operative gesture would be greeted. At last, the criminal in front of me having accomplished her evil designs, I arrived at the front of the queue and paid my money to the female cashier, a girl who looked as if she might have just passed her ninth birthday.

Then, with what I considered to be rather suave nonchalance, I proceeded to co-operate.

'Oh, by the way,' I said, 'there's a big jar of Piccalilli all over the floor round the corner there, in the pickle aisle. I just thought – you know – I ought to tell you.'

Without a single word or change of expression the girl jabbed her thumb against the button beside her. A bell rang somewhere in the distance. She waited, her eyes wide with bored vacancy. I had the uncomfortable feeling that I had ceased to exist. Eventually, a young man wearing a little green trilby and a bow-tie of similar shade arrived at the till with an expression of mechanical enquiry on his face. He was much older than the girl – fifteen at least judging by his moustache.

'What?' he said.

The girl spoke, her words emerging in little leaden lumps of weary exasperation.

'Customer complainin' about a breakage in the pickle aisle.'

The young man, clearly a master of verbal economy, emitted a single grunt, which managed to express annoyance, impatience, and scornful distaste for the whole pathetic customer race. He started to move away.

In most situations of this kind I am rendered impotent by the disease of politeness. Sometimes, when our car comes back from the garage in as bad or worse condition than it went in, I swear to my wife that *this* time I'm really going to give them a piece of my mind.

'This time', I snarl, 'they're going to get the rough edge of my tongue! I'm going straight up there and I'm gonna tell 'em!'

Breathing threats and imprecations I stride up to the garage full of angry lion-like confidence. As I walk in through the door, though, something happens. I turn into a sheep.

'Hello, there!' I bleat cheerily, 'the old car's playing up again. Not your fault, of course. I just wondered if I could pay you some more money to fix it again. Ha-ha-ha! What a silly old life, eh . . .?'

This time it was different. I was too annoyed to be polite. I wanted my warm gratitude.

'Excuse me!' I said, catching up with him, 'I wasn't complaining, I was co-operating. It says up there' – I pointed – 'that you will be warmly grateful to customers who report breakages or spillage in the aisles. That's what I've done. Now, how about a bit of warm gratitude?'

He stared at me for a moment, searching for words with which to seal this unexpected breach in the surrounding wall of his small world. His reply, when it came, was triumphant.

'Well, you don't have to clear it up, do you?'

So stunned was I by this startling piece of non-logic that I couldn't think of anything else to say.

'Breakage in the pickle aisle!'

The cry rang out from the bow-tied one, and was taken up and passed on with ever-decreasing volume until it could be heard only very faintly somewhere in the bowels of the shop. Finally, a diminutive member of the shop staff (probably a university student on vacation) arrived with a selection of cleaning implements and attacked the problem, muttering as he did so about 'people who make trouble for other people'.

'So who,' I asked myself later, 'actually meant what was said on that sign over the tills?'

Perhaps if the managing director of Crossroads had been present when I 'co-operated', he might have shaken me by the hand and formally thanked me on behalf of the board of directors for my wonderfully public-spirited act. But he wasn't there, and clearly no one else was prepared to represent him.

I fear that many churches have exactly the same problem as that branch of Crossroads. The huge sign that hangs over the church – the Bible – promises love and healing and adventure and miracles and dynamism and involvement in an urgent rescue operation. Too often it is impossible to find people who will represent the promises that Jesus made. He still keeps those promises in all who genuinely follow him. How sad that so many outsiders who venture past the portals of their local church are greeted with the equivalent of that young shopworker's query – 'What?'

We'd better be careful. Our managing director will make his next visit without any warning.

Happiness

Can we expect to find lasting happiness?

I'm afraid this is not a subject that my family readily associates with the grumpy recluse who squats in his caravan at the bottom of the garden, getting more and more irritable as he tries and fails to write something funny. From a distance, I am told, I look like a caged muppet.

The gap between public and private presentation has always been a problem for Christian communicators.

My wife, Bridget, for instance, is all too aware that she is married to an average Christian whose job happens to involve exposure to the public through books and broadcasting and speaking

engagements of various kinds. Those of us who
do stand on platforms to bleat at others tend to get
a bit carried away at times. We are so anxious to
give God a good reference, as it were, and so
fearful that the humble crumbs of our Christian
experience will not be sufficiently nourishing for
the baby birds who wait, open mouthed, to be fed,
that we inflate the truth, not realising that in the
process it may become hollow and insubstantial.
At least, that's what happens to me, and the
temptation is upon me again today, even as I
write this.

Can we find lasting happiness?

'Of course we can!' whispers the neurotic professional Christian in me. 'Tell 'em! Tell 'em! All
you have to do is ask Jesus into your life, pray,
read the Bible, go to church, be nice to your

mother and you'll be happy for ever and ever, amen, hallelujah, praise the Lord! Go on – tell 'em! You'll be letting God down if you don't!'

But a moment's reflection suggests that I'll be letting God down if I do. I know lots of Christians, all of varying denominational shapes and sizes, each one a different, but essential part of the body of Christ; some of them, me included perhaps, those 'odd parts' that Paul talks about in Corinthians.

Now, if I'm absolutely honest, the thing that all these people have in common is *not* happiness. Many of them, an awful lot of them, are living and trying to cope with hurts, and problems in relationships, and illness, and doubt, and conflict, and personal failure, just as much as they are enjoying the more positive aspects of life and faith. Of course it may just be that I happen to know a particularly unfortunate load of Christians – but I don't think so. The thing they do have in common is that they are human beings who are trying to follow Jesus.

Let us look at Jesus for a moment – God, but also a human being, who was once described as 'a man of sorrows'. It is a matter of record that Jesus experienced grief, anger, hunger, weariness and, when the disciples failed to stay awake at Gethsemane, a profound disappointment that they had let him down. Again at Gethsemane, he sweated drops of blood as he agonised over the choice between life, which must have seemed very sweet to him, and a horrible death, for him the inevitable consequence of obedience. Later, on the cross, Jesus learned for the first time in his life what rejection and despair really meant.

'My God, my God, why have you forsaken me?' can hardly be described as the cry of a happy man.

The apostle Paul fared no better. In the course of his ministry to the Gentiles he was shipwrecked, imprisoned, starved, beaten, reviled and finally executed – probably beheaded by his Roman captors. Stephen was stoned to death. Peter was crucified upside down – at his own request.

Leaping the centuries to our own time, I have a friend called Mike, a Christian, who was recently married for the second time. His first marriage failed largely through his wife's inability to accept the inconveniences and demands of a successful acting career. She left him eventually and later they were divorced. Mike was devastated by this failure, and not at all comforted by the fact that, whereas God seemed happy to extend forgiveness to all concerned, some of his fellow worshippers certainly didn't. He changed churches, and a couple of years later fell in love with and married his present wife. Very shortly after their wedding she developed a chronically debilitating form of arthritis which has prevented her from working or walking without the aid of sticks ever since. Not a happy situation on the face of it. Rather, the contrary.

My friend Philip Illot, an anglo-Catholic priest whose biography I have been privileged to write, has suffered throughout his life. Through his ministry people have been healed, miracles have happened, amazing events have been witnessed; yet he has gone through a succession of appalling experiences beginning with abuse as a small child, and continuing to this day with emotional and physical trauma and hardship that are in stark contrast with the relief and healing he has so often brought to other people.

Now, before we go any further, I'm well aware that certain spiritual brothers and sisters, particularly, perhaps, members of that fast-growing denomination 'The Holy and Apostolic True Church of the Abundant Revelation of Living Stones' will be just aching to tell me a) that Jesus, Paul, Stephen, Peter, my friend Mike, and Philip Illot must have experienced plenty of happy occasions as well as the rotten ones – well, that's probably true; and b) that even when they *were* feeling unhappy, a sense of inner joy, the joy of the Lord, would have been present at the same time. This response has become one of the greatest and most oft-repeated clichés of the Christian faith, and, like most clichés, it has its roots in the truth. Jesus is quoted in John's gospel as saying: 'Peace I leave with you; my peace I give to you; not as the world gives do I give to you. Let not your hearts be troubled, neither let them be afraid.'

Jesus was offering the 'shalom' peace, that sense of well-being and wholeness that comes from the knowledge that one loves and is loved by God; a peace that cannot be disturbed by worldly hardship or suffering; and, as countless folk can

74

witness, it really does exist, and it really can sustain our spirits inwardly when things get rough on the outside. The problem with the clichéd, simplistic expression of this great truth, is that there are times in the lives of nearly all the Christians I know when suffering is so intense or prolonged that they lose their peace and have to fly, as it were, on automatic pilot. Whether or not this ought to be a fact isn't very relevant, because it *is* a fact. People *do* get troubled, and they *do* become afraid. At such times they are not happy.

The answer to our original query about lasting happiness may lie in the consideration of two other questions:

(1) Why do people continue to follow Jesus *despite* suffering and unhappiness, and (2) What, ideally, does following him really mean?

The answer to the first question seems to lie in relationship. Jesus endured the sorrows and agonies of the world, not out of theological or nationalistic loyalty, not because of some vague personal philosophy about the efficacy of suffering, and not only because of the benefits that his death and resurrection would bring to mankind; but because, with a passion too deep for us to comprehend, he really did love his father so much that he was prepared to be obedient way, way beyond the point where it started to hurt. In his heart he knew that lasting happiness lay in the perfect preservation of a relationship that meant everything to him.

About his disciples he prayed: 'Father, I desire that they also whom thou hast given me, may be with me where I am' and therein, I suggest, lies the motivation for Paul, Stephen, Peter, my friend Mike and his wife, and Philip Illot. They are all prepared to follow Jesus to the place where he is, through failure, triumph, ecstasy, despair, certainty and doubt, not because they are driven by a misty, theoretical religious instinct, but because, in the end, they want to be with him; and they want to be with him because they love him and are fascinated by him; and they know that, ultimately, it is only with Jesus that lasting happiness will be found.

My friend, Mike, for instance, tells me that although his wife's illness is a heavy burden for them both to bear, and although it does cause them both a lot of unhappiness, their relationship with each other and with Jesus is such that their over-all calm and optimism is quite inexplicable to those who see only the tragedy in their situation.

The answer to the second question, about what following really means, might be divided into 'doing', and 'being with'.

What do I mean by 'doing'?

I fear that modern pharisaism, like ancient pharisaism, would have us believe that the Christian approach to life is a very negative one – a list of don'ts. And, of course, Jesus did make it abundantly clear that God hates sin and finds any and every expression of it totally unacceptable. But Jesus' entry into the world brought Grace, and a new perspective on the problem of sin.

In the twenty-second chapter of Matthew's gospel we find Jesus lopping off the negative commandments from the original ten, to leave only two – the ones that begin with the words 'Thou shalt. . . .'

'Thou shalt love the Lord thy God with all thy heart and with all thy soul and with all thy mind.' And secondly: 'Thou shalt love thy neighbour as thyself.'

'On these two commandments,' says Jesus, 'depend all the law and the prophets.'

In other words, the 'shalt nots' are swallowed up in the 'shalts'. Later in the same book he tells the parable of the sheep and the goats. The sheep get into heaven because they have visited the sick and imprisoned, clothed the naked and fed the hungry, not because they have not got drunk, or not fornicated, or not been covetous. The positive Gospel of Jesus Christ says that we will be justified by our faith in him, and that *that* faith will result in us doing things on God's behalf for the benefit of others. Constant, neurotic, spiritual and moral self-analysis is not usually very relevant in this context. The narrow path that Jesus speaks of elsewhere is the way of loving, caring – doing. Sins are the seductive gateways off the path on to the broad and easy road of not loving, not caring, doing nothing.

As well as the 'doing' there is the 'being with'. We shall not want to follow Jesus unless we know him well enough to think him worth following. I'm talking about prayer, but a great deal of prayer is simply friendship, and God desires our friendship more than we can imagine. Having said that, I know only too well how prayer and Bible study can become dry and difficult to maintain. That is a whole other subject really, and a very important one, but there is one practical way of establishing or re-establishing this friendship with God, that has worked for a lot of people.

Take the gospels – or one of the gospels, John perhaps – clear your mind as much as you possibly can of everything you thought you knew about what Jesus did or said, then read the book and find out what he really *did* say and do. The result can be quite a shock, and if you keep your spiritual ears open you may be surprised at how much the Holy Spirit speaks to you through your discoveries. If you feel you want to answer back, and a dialogue gets going – well, you're praying.

Someone once said that we should pray as if prayer was the only thing that worked, then work as if work was the only thing that worked. It sounds a pretty good recipe to me, as long as we allow some space for a few miracles.

I doubt whether most of us are able truly to find lasting happiness in this world. There are those who, either because of their particular temperament or because they walk specially closely with God, enjoy a consistent contentment and peace. They make wonderfully good ambassadors for the Christian faith; but I also believe that for all of us, at our different stages and in our different states, it is possible, between and around and through the trials and tribulations that beset us, to taste the joy of heaven, and that there, in heaven, our happiness will be unalloyed and eternal.

I must confess that I get very low sometimes; that's the effect of my temperament; but when people say to me, 'How can you be so low when you're a Christian? Why don't you abandon Jesus?' my response is very similar to that of the disciples two thousand years ago when all but that small band had deserted him.

'Where else would I go? He has the words of eternal life – and happiness.'

Football
Joe

No one who witnessed it in 1989 will ever forget
the disaster in the Hillsborough Football Stadium
when ninety-five people were crushed to death.
One of them was a ten-year-old boy. There must
have been many fathers who like me, on that
awful day, looked at their own ten-year-old sons
and appreciated their value even more than
before.

My Joseph was ten at the time. He was, and still
is, definitely a one-off. Joe is a quirky, sensitive
character, full of complicated thoughts and feelings, but not a great chatterer like the others,
until you get him on his own, that is. He's not as
physically demonstrative as the other three

either, perhaps, but when he does come and put his arms round you and kiss you on the cheek, it feels like an enormous privilege, something really special.

Joe eats, sleeps and breathes football. He plays it, he watches it, he has an encyclopaedic knowledge of it that is far in advance of my own. He happens to support Manchester United (a team some of you may have heard of), but it's the game of football itself that he loves more than any individual team. On the Saturday of the Hillsborough tragedy, at tea-time, our family prayed for everyone who was bereaved or hurt by the things that happened at the Liverpool-Nottingham Forest match, and Joe's 'amen' came straight from the heart. He cared.

The other thing about Joe is that, like my other children, he's done more to help me understand myself in relation to God than almost anyone or anything else. Take the whole business of repairing friendship, for instance. I love Joe very much, but he's capable of making me more angry than just about anyone in the entire world. I suspect that's because he's not able to pretend or play games about relationships. He just responds as he feels, and if I've been very busy, or away from home a lot, he tends to retreat into himself and present me with a rather blank face and a total absence of those special cuddles that I mentioned earlier. If I'm feeling guilty about my absorption in activities that take up family time, I'm quite likely to get very angry when this happens. If the pattern is then repeated a few times my relationship – my friendship – with Joe dries up almost completely. It just atrophies. And then, somehow, the friendship has to be repaired. The question is – how?

Now, you can't buy Joe's goodwill with *things*. You could present him with bicycles, radios, stereo units, footballs, anything you like. He'd accept them and enjoy having them like any kid of his age, but it wouldn't restore the relationship. So that's no good.

Another thing that doesn't work is cheap, brief expressions of affection or interest in the world that he specially inhabits. Taking a few seconds out of one's busy life to communicate a superficial involvement in Joe's preoccupations cuts no ice at all.

This presents particular problems to people like me who, unfortunately, tend towards manipulative control of others as opposed to wholehearted involvement. We learn our 'tricks' young, and it can be quite a shock to discover that the ones we usually find most useful, are no use at all with folk like Joe.

Take sulking for instance.

Sulking doesn't work with Joe. He doesn't notice it. This is a shame, because if there's one thing I'm an expert in, it's making other people feel guilty when I've done something wrong. If ever sulking is included in the catalogue of Olympic sports I'm pretty well guaranteed a place on the winners' podium. Gold or silver medal at the very least.

I'm particularly proud of a rather fine shuddering sigh that's taken some years to perfect. When timed correctly it can actually confuse my wife into apologising to me for something that *I've* done! It hints at deep, incalculable hurt, or secret knowledge of impending tragedy, bravely borne for the sake of others. I have toyed with the idea of patenting this effect and instructing others in its use, possibly by correspondence course – it really is *so* effective, but it only works with selected people, and Joe is definitely not one of them.

Anger is a waste of time. It has the effect of reducing tension in me, but it makes no real impact on him, he simply retreats even further into himself and the situation is then worse than before.

There's only one way to repair a friendship with Joe. I know – I've done it a few times now. You have to go right into his world, committed to using plenty of what is nowadays called 'Prime Time' to be with him, genuinely involved with his interests, proving how much you value him by abandoning distractions for a significant period.

In practice this usually means a Saturday spent going into the local town – Eastbourne in our case – having lunch in some cafe, looking round the shops together, buying one or two quite small things, and talking *properly*; Joe chats like mad when you take him out on his own. What it really amounts to is just being together in a *real* way. One day like this is usually enough to get things back on a proper footing. After that it's a matter of ensuring that regular genuine contact is happening.

I realised some time ago that my relationship with God is very similar. It's no good me moaning about feeling separated from him if I'm not spending prime time with him; talking to him; listening to him; showing I love him enough to get involved. You can't buy God's friendship with good works. Superficiality, sulking and anger are no use. God is like Joe. He wants me to make real friends with him. It can be costly (it is with Joe), and I don't always manage it by any means, but I can tell you that it makes all the difference in the world.

The Inter-Denominational World Cup

With a house full of football fanatics like mine, 1990 was inevitably a very significant year. World Cup fever gripped most of us for the duration of the tournament in Italy.

To celebrate this major event, I include the following report on a rather less well-known tournament:

Commentator: Good evening and welcome to the inter-denominational football cup. We're halfway through the competition now; and we've already had some marvellous encounters in this exciting seven-a-side tournament.

Beginning with a sparkling

contest between the Strict and Particular Baptists – they're the ones who insist on showering before the match – and the lenient and not very fussy at all Baptists – they're the ones who would shower if they could remember what it was for in the first place.

Fascinating during that match to look around the arena and see other teams limbering up and waiting for their matches to begin. The Greenbelt team dribbling quietly in the corner, one of the Roman Catholic substitutes being given the reserve sacrament over at the rail, and John Wimber being offered a contract by one of the English teams; he doesn't quite know what's going on, he just signs and wonders. It's all happening here tonight.

The following match was a real humdinger between the Spring Harvest side – four centres but very little defence – and the anglo-catholic team, whose game is based largely on the use of high crosses and some very ornate set-pieces. The Spring Harvest side took an early lead after Graham Kendrick took the ball the length of the pitch, shouting 'Make way!

Make way!', but the anglo-catholics fought back in the second half, assisted by the wind and the fact that they were now playing in the direction of Rome.

Other matches: The Church of England versus Methodist battle was postponed because, although the captains agreed on the rules, the other team members weren't so sure. Once they did get going it was dazzling stuff, except at the point when the Church of England captain stopped to read the notices just as a goal was about to be scored. Shortly after that one of the players was injured – Colin Urquhart ran on to the pitch with a wet sponge (unidentified as yet), only to be told by the injured Methodist that he wasn't sure he was ready yet for Revival.

The Pentecostal team, who reached the tournament finals by a process of Elim-ination, managed to overcome the House Church team, and were ecstatic. Experts agreed that the House Church side would have done a lot better if they hadn't all played with their arms in the air and their eyes closed. They were also penalised twice for moving the goalposts and marching around the edge of the pitch claiming victory for the Lord.

Impressive combination play by the U.R.C. team, although they were disqualified in the end for dangerous and illegal use of zimmers. A pity this, as they would have easily defeated the Bishop of Durham's private team, which, despite hard work and some very fancy footwork, scored a number of own goals, and insisted that the referee was only present in a symbolic sense.

The Famous Christian team, very popular here tonight, especially at the moment when their captain, Cliff Richard, after spending much of the evening shooting wide of the posts, sang frustratedly into his opponents' goal:

'But these miss-you nights are the longest . . .'

Terrific cheering now as the next match gets under way, and it could be a rather difficult one, two anglican synod sides, one in favour of allowing women to play, and the other not. The Archbishop of Canterbury, amazingly, attempting to captain both teams.

(LOUD CHEERS)

Great excitement here behind me! Let's find out what's going on from one of the supporters. (APPROACHES ONE) Why the big cheer?

Supporter: (WITH RABID EXCITE-MENT) Yeah, one of the synod teams just passed a resolution agreeing in principle that a passing movement would be initiated, that might, in the context of

	sensitive awareness of popular response, eventually culminate in the scoring of a goal!
Commentator:	Electrifying! Well, that's where we have to leave it, I'm afraid. The final? Well, predictions suggest a clash between the fundamentalists and the liberals and that's one that's bound to be settled in the midfield. A final comment, endorsed by the managing director of our sponsor – Divine Products. Remember that denominations is an anagram of 'not made in Sion'. Goodnight.

A Professional Foul

There seems to be a fashion nowadays for exploding popular myths about famous events and people, past or present, living or dead. You know the sort of thing I mean, don't you?

The gunfight at the O.K. Corral was actually a game of tiddly-winks.

Genghis Khan was a home-loving, gentle type, with a talent for social work.

St Francis of Assisi regularly used his bird-charming skills to assemble the ingredients for pigeon pie.

No doubt scholarship will soon reveal that Winston Churchill was a German spy, Columbus was a chronic agoraphobic, Florence Nightingale was a poisoner, and Jack the Ripper's murders were definitely committed by Queen Victoria, sneaking around the East End on stilts with a bag full of knives.

Public figures are observed and examined by the Media of this age in a way that was impossible previously. Perhaps our discovery that nearly all idols have feet of clay has produced a sort of corporate resentment in us. If we can't have the kind of heroes that we want, then we're jolly well going to debunk all the ones that previous generations ignorantly elevated to super-star status!

Nevertheless, we still preserve a small stock of present-day heroes, and, presumably because they are few in number, we get very upset when our respect or admiration is shown to be misplaced.

Take the case of a certain professional footballer, famed as a Manchester United and England player, but also highly respected for an on-pitch behaviour record that was not blemished by a single instance of either being sent off or displaying rowdy behaviour – a real gentleman of the game.

Then, one morning, a daily newspaper devoted most of its back page to reporting a public statement by this same player, in which he stated quite openly that when a (euphemistically termed) 'professional foul' was the only way to stop an opposing player, he did not hesitate to use it. (A professional foul is one where a piece of deliberately illegal behaviour is disguised so as to appear blameless.)

This honest admission produced quite a reaction, not just from the footballing establishment, but from ordinary supporters as well. People like their heroes intact. This is, of course, very unfair on any ordinary human being – perfect people are rather few and far between.

I happened to be travelling on a train from London to Polegate when I read this 'shock-horror' revelation, and as I finished the article, I folded my newspaper, put it on the seat beside me, and gazed out of the window, lost in thought.

Leaving aside the ins and outs and rights and wrongs of the particular instance I had just read about, what, I wondered, were the kinds of 'professional foul' or its equivalent that I used in my own life? How might other people's perceptions of me change, if I opened up in the way that this footballer had done?

I don't think it would be appropriate to describe here some of the grimmer little ploys that I recognised as vices I had managed to disguise as virtues. Not that there weren't any. On the contrary, there were far too many. Even so, as I stepped off the train at Polegate Station, I felt that I had not quite identified any incident in my own life which paralleled the concept of the professional foul with *absolute* accuracy.

Still pondering this matter, I walked out into the station forecourt intending to engage one of the taxis that were usually queuing for customers when the London train came in. This time there was only one cab available, standing by the TAXI sign about fifty yards away. Between me and the sign there was just one person, an elderly lady moving very slowly with the aid of a stick in the same direction as me.

Somehow I *knew* that the elderly lady was heading for that solitary taxi, but I made an instant decision to pretend to myself and her and God and anyone else who might be interested, that I didn't really know that at all. After all, it was perfectly feasible that she was heading for the car park to pick up her own vehicle, wasn't it? How was I to know what she was doing? I wasn't a mind reader, was I?

Briskly overtaking my tottering competitor I reached the taxi and put my hand on the door handle. Suddenly I seemed to see an ethereal yellow card raised in the back of my mind.

A professional foul! Never mind how feasible anything was. My conscious intention was to do something selfish and deceptive. Remaining publicly intact was not the point at all. Removing my hand from the door I waited for the old lady to arrive, and helped her into the taxi. Just as I closed the door another cab drove into the forecourt and swept round the circular space to take up its position beside the TAXI sign. Gratefully, I settled into the passenger seat and was soon heading for home.

So, the business with the old lady and the first taxi hadn't really mattered after all, I mused, as we sped along the A22 towards Hailsham.

But of course it *had* mattered. The more I thought about that little incident, the more important it seemed. It had forced me to ask myself how many other times I had played this kind of game with my public and private morality. And, most significantly of all, perhaps, I realised that my sense of the reality of God's presence in my life was insufficient to prevent me from committing the kind of inward sins that are akin to the professional foul. Did I honestly think that God would be as easily taken in by my public posing as those people who were unable to see inside my head?

I am beginning to realise that openness with God and Man is not an optional extra. It's better to 'come clean' and admit that, whereas God is perfect, I'm not. I think I shall make a point of exploding my own myth before someone else blows the whistle on me.

Criticism

I have only ever once interrupted a sermon. It isn't an activity I would recommend or advocate, but perhaps it doesn't happen quite as often as it should. On this occasion, the speaker was talking about the Christian approach to personal finance, and the question of H.P. agreements in particular. This is, of course, very much in line with the current obsession with tidying up every aspect of something called 'The Christian Life'. I haven't yet seen any paperbacks entitled 'Loo-flushing the Christian way', or 'Pencil-sharpening in the Spirit', but I don't doubt they are being prepared at this very moment.

This time, though, it was the old 'never-never'

system for buying household and personal goods, that was under the microscope. In general, said the speaker, it was best for Christians to avoid transactions of this kind. Debt was debt, whether it was formally organised or not. Much better, he added, to buy what you can afford, using money you've actually got. I sensed a little shadow of guilt settling over my friend, Brenda, sitting next to me. I knew her very well. She lived on the nearby council estate, in a house that was almost exclusively furnished and equipped with goods bought on hire purchase. I knew for a fact that she was still paying for her washing machine and cooker. I could almost hear her brain clicking as she computed the sum of her debts. She laid a hand on my arm, and leaned towards my ear.

'Adrian,' she whispered, 'I owe close on three hundred quid for my stuff!'

Brenda only needs a little shove to make her leap into the black abyss of guilt. Years ago she lost all respect for herself, and the rehabilitation of her self-worth has been a long, slow process. God is doing it, but the job may not be completed this side of heaven. A thought struck me. I raised my arm quickly before I could lose my nerve.

'Excuse me, sorry to interrupt, but you didn't actually mention mortgages. I mean – you've got a mortgage, haven't you? So have I. We owe thousands and thousands of pounds between us, don't we? It's just a huge, glorified H.P. system really – don't you think?'

Mortgages, it appeared, were 'different'. Never mind. I could feel Brenda's shadow lifting. *She* had got the point.

But why didn't mortgages count? Why are people so easily able to see areas that need correction in other people's lives, and remain blind to similar problems in their own? In the case I've just mentioned, it's probably something to do with an illusion that frequently bedevils the Church; namely, that a very organised and materially successful life indicates spiritual solidity. It is interesting to note how those who are socially and financially 'Inferior', can become victims of an oddly predatory form of – so-called – ministry, from a certain type of 'successful' Christian.

Even more common, though, is that form of modern pharisaism where Christians home in on satisfactorily visible things, such as smoking and drinking, despite their inability to face invisible, non-public vices or sins in themselves. (I hasten to add, incidentally, that I don't consider smoking or drinking to be sins in themselves.) Occasionally, however, the fault-finder can come badly unstuck, as when, some years ago, a gentleman challenged a friend of mine about his pipe-smoking habit.

'I'm surprised at you,' he said, 'a Christian like you carrying on with a filthy habit like that!'

My friend has a *real* gift of knowledge; not the sort where you offer vague comfort in sixteenth-century English, but a specific, relevant, sometimes disturbingly accurate insight into unseen things. He looked keenly at the man who had spoken.

'Well,' he replied calmly, 'it's a lot better than *your* filthy habit.'

The erstwhile critic blushed to the roots of his hair, and departed hastily. My friend hadn't the faintest idea what the 'filthy habit' might be, but clearly the Holy Spirit had hit the nail right on the head.

I have been judgemental in just about every way that's possible at one time or another, but I specialise in something that I call 'The Spiritual Three-Step'. One of the steps is forward, and the other two are back. The 'dance' goes something like this.

For a long time, possibly days, or weeks, or months, or even years, I wrestle with, worry about, or live with, being spiritually low. It may be because of a particular issue, or it may be a whole set of problems. Then, one day, through prayer, or advice, or reading, or just growing up a little more, my chronic lowness is overcome, and I discover, to my intense relief, that I am experiencing a little of the joy and peace that Christians are 'supposed' to enjoy all the time. For a while, all I feel is a deep and honest gratitude to God for bringing me out of the pit. This is the one step forward.

What happens next, however, is that I feel a burning desire to advertise my 'rightness' with God. I start to tell people, patiently but firmly, that they need to 'get right with the Lord'. I avoid mention of the fact that I have only just found peace myself, but I do make it clear through my crinkly smile and other-worldly manner, that my own state is one of healthy spirituality. These are the two steps backwards. In my old gloomy state, I might have been a bit of a wet blanket, but at least I was recognisable as a human being. Now I am that most oppressive of beings, the Christian who is as incapable of normal communication when he is spiritually high, as he is incapable of normal participation when he is low. Pray for Christians like us who follow this kind of manic-depressive pattern. We need it! We are forever lecturing others about the sins and weaknesses that are all too familiar to us. The tendency is psychological and temperamental rather than spiritual, and it can be very destructive.

Why are we Christians so critical and condemnatory of each other at times? Often, it is the result of fear and insecurity. When children are left to organise themselves in situations where an adult would normally be in charge, they have a tendency to create rules and restrictions that are far harsher and less flexible than under the adult regime. Where there is fundamental lack of belief, this happens among Christian families and churches as well. Groups will develop a rigid structure of do's and don'ts, to protect themselves from the uncertainties and risks involved in grappling with the real world. Anyone who breaks one of the rules is threatening the security of the group, and must therefore be corrected or rejected.

This is understandable, but it has very little to do with the ideal outlook as Jesus taught it. He himself was a totally released and free person, one hundred per cent against sin, and one hundred per cent *for* the sinful individuals with whom he was so tender and forgiving. His most intense vituperation was reserved for the hypocrites – church leaders who burdened others with endless rules and regulations, and did nothing to relieve those burdens. The Christians I've met who walk closely with God don't make me feel bad. They make me feel as if I could be good. Their breadth and positivity have a creative, life-changing effect. They are like Jesus.

We are called to be '*doers*', not narrow-eyed guardians of a complex system of laws. Sin is more easily displaced than guarded against. Perhaps if our churches opened up to the world and the Spirit in a bolder way we would discover that there is an adventure with God waiting for us, that is far more exciting than sin, and a thousand times more useful than the detection of faults in our brothers and sisters. God will judge us all in time. Meanwhile, let's be positive. Let's look for the best in others, and let's not inhibit the spread of God's Kingdom by concentrating on the rulebook. We are only truly safe if we let go. The avoidance of sin on its own is safe but sterile. Where it is accompanied or made possible by *extravagant* goodness, it can change the world.

They don't smoke, but neither do they breathe fresh air very deeply
They don't drink wine, but neither do they enjoy lemonade; they don't swear, but neither do they glory in any magnificent words, neither poetry nor prayer;
They don't gamble, but neither do they take much chance on God;
They don't look at women and girls with lust in their hearts, but neither do they roll breathless with love and laughter, naked under the sun of high summer.
It's all rather pale and round-shouldered, the great Prince lying in prison.

George Target

Confession
Thou Shalt Not Eavesdrop

I suppose this book wouldn't be truly complete unless I included at least a couple of grovelling confessions. Well, here's one, and I hope you like it.

I am an inveterate eavesdropper. Not just because I happen to be a writer who is constantly scavenging for material (although I always think that sounds a wonderfully smooth excuse, don't you?) but because I really am fascinated by real conversation between real people in day-to-day situations.

I've been dropping eaves anywhere and everywhere for years and years. I'm the rather good-looking – all right, ordinary-looking, if you want to be boringly accurate – man with a beard, apparently deeply absorbed in his newspaper, sitting just in front of you on the bus.

Don't worry – you can carry on exchanging hissed imprecations with your spouse. I'm not listening. Well, you'd never guess that I was listening, anyway. Actually I can hear every exasperated word you and your beloved say. When you get off in a minute I might even make a few notes on the back of an envelope.

One good row could be a whole chapter in my next-but-one book – if I pad my jottings out to five thousand words, and set the whole thing in Russia, and make the fate of the Western world hang on its outcome.

Rather an honour for you, I should have thought; especially when you consider that the original argument was about whether the dog got fed or not before you came out.

Is eavesdropping a sin? I don't honestly know. 'Thou shalt not eavesdrop.'

It sounds a little odd, doesn't it? But until a blinding revelation convicts me unequivocally, I shall continue with my earwigging activities. After all, I can always repent later, can't I?

To be honest, most of the things you overhear are not very dramatic. Discussions, rows, jokes, gossipy chats – they're all interesting. But they don't have much 'shock value', if you know what I mean. That's why it was so exceptional one day when a mere snatch of dialogue overheard in a station buffet, chilled me to the narrow, and left me feeling deeply disturbed long after the initial impact had passed.

It doesn't matter when it was, except that it wasn't too long after the Press and TV news had been full of accounts of soccer violence at home and abroad.

The two people involved were very ordinary. One was the girl who worked behind the buffet counter, the other was a young British Rail employee, probably in his late teens or early twenties, quite unexceptional to look at, both of them.

They obviously knew each other. Being genuinely absorbed in my newspaper for once, I didn't register the first part of the conversation, but the bit I did hear went like this.

'Still livin' in the same place, Gary?'

'Yeah, but I'm movin' soon.'

'Oh, where you goin' then?'

'Movin' up to live with a mate at the other end of town.'

'Oh, why's that then, Gary?'

'It's better. There's more aggro up that way. . . .'

This last, stunning announcement was delivered in precisely the same tone that someone else might use to talk about superior housing or better recreational facilities.

In a modern, but not less grotesque version of the old werewolf legend, this young man called Gary was an inoffensive – probably very helpful – employee of British Rail by day, and a committed seeker after 'aggro' by night.

When evil is deep and uncompromising and consistent, it's somehow easier to face and combat. When, as in the case of Gary and his associates, something like violence has been elevated to the status of legitimate recreation – albeit within a limited social group – and can be mentioned casually as a desirable attribute of the area in which one plans to live, it's much harder to establish where the real spiritual battleground is.

This seems to me one of the most successful devil's ploys of this age. When the edges between black and white, evil and good, wrong and right, are blurred and confusing, we can end up spiritually paralysed, vaguely feeling that to do nothing is better than doing the wrong thing.

Now, more than ever, we need to make our priority a close walk with God, asking for *his* wisdom, and keeping our ears wide open. Sometimes our willingness to *listen* can make all the difference.

A friend of mine told the story recently of a girl who was counselling an older woman, when the words 'God hates mummies and daddies' came into her mind. Very wisely she refrained from immediately passing on this strange piece of information. 'Words from the Lord' can so easily turn out to be the product of wishful thinking or an over-active imagination. You know the sort of thing I mean:

'I saw, as it were, a frying pan, and within the pan did appear an egg, shaped like unto the land of Greenland, and behold the egg did speak . . . etc.'

You really do have to be very careful. The girl in this case talked and prayed about the words in question with a friend whom she respected and trusted. They decided that the message was from God, and with considerable trepidation the counsellor returned to the lady she had been trying to help and repeated the sentence that had come into her mind. To her consternation the woman collapsed in tears, explaining when she recovered that, as a young girl, she had been continually abused by her uncle who always prefaced his unwelcome advances with the words: 'Let's play mummies and daddies. . . .'

After many years the Holy Spirit had, at last, found someone whose ears were wide open enough to hear words that would bring the sympathy of God to a life that had been crippled by past hurts.

It's always worth trying to overhear what the Holy Spirit is saying. He doesn't mind us eavesdropping at all.

Political Repentance

Another confession.

I have not been political, and I repent.

My parents always voted Liberal if they voted at all, but I suspect that their understanding of politics was less than profound. I remember asking them to tell me the difference between the three major parties. As far as I can recall, they said that the Conservatives wanted to keep everything the same as it was now, the Labour Party wanted to abolish rich people, and the Liberals wanted to be fair to everybody.

This may of course be a more penetrating political analysis than appears at first sight, but at the time it failed to inspire me with any burning interest in the activities of politicians. As I grew older I learned how to conceal my ignorance beneath a thin veneer of sceptical derision.

'Naturally', my attitude seemed to imply, 'I'm pretty shrewd about the whole business, but if you understood it like I do, you'd know that it's really not worth bothering with.'

In fact, it was only fairly recently that I was jerked out of this absurd false complacency. It was during a period when my life had settled into a pattern of rather cosy little routines, one of which took me to London each week.

Every Wednesday morning during the early part of that year I caught a train at 6.30 from Polegate in East Sussex to Victoria Station, London. After a short but crowded journey by tube to Oxford Circus, I walked up Regent Street to a small sandwich cafe on the right, just before you come to the St George's Hotel and All Souls, Langham Place.

There, I ordered a black coffee and a bacon sandwich – made with brown bread and no butter because I was dieting – and read whichever magazine or newspaper I'd picked up at the station bookstall.

At about 8.50 I sighed heavily, folded my paper, paid the bill and walked round the corner to Broadcasting House. There I collected an admission sticker from reception and descended into the bowels of the building via two flights of steps.

Fifty yards or so along the corridor I pushed through two swing doors and found myself in the control room attached to Derek Jameson's 'bunker', the studio from which Radio Two's 7.30-9.30 programme is broadcast. A few minutes later I was sitting opposite Derek delivering my prepared script for the slot entitled 'Pause For Thought'.

What has all this got to do with not being political?

Well, typically, I was so absorbed in my own cosy little routine and the contribution I would be making, it never occurred to me that I might be challenged by something someone else was talking about.

Derek was conducting a series of phone-in voting opportunities on topical issues. The one that really penetrated my thick skull was concerned with the building of the Channel Tunnel between England and France – not where the rail link should run or anything like that, but whether it should be built at all.

The response was enormous, and the result unequivocal. The vast majority of people just didn't want it – as simple as that.

As I sat on the south-bound train later, I chewed this over in my mind and realised I didn't want the tunnel either. In fact I *hated* the idea of it. Not 'as a Christian' – I'm sure there isn't a correct Christian view of such an issue – but because on some very deep level I wanted Great Britain to keep its island status.

I didn't – and don't – want to be physically joined to the continent of Europe.

As my train flew past East Croydon and rattled through Gatwick I got angrier and angrier. By the time I got to my home station of Polegate I had a whole list of complaints going back several years, all concerned with valuable things sacrificed on the alter of efficiency.

'Just think,' I stormed at Bridget when I got home, 'all those things they've done without asking me!'

'Such as?' she asked dispassionately.

'Steam trains!' I replied. 'They got rid of them and brought in boring old diesels and non-corridor carriages and they never asked me!'

'But they were dirty and – '

'Currency!' I cried. 'While I wasn't looking they got rid of our lovely, curly, complicated pounds, shillings and pence and put nasty metallic, robotic, rotten old decimal currency in its place – scandalous!'

'But the children find it much – '

'I turn my back for a moment, and they abolish Rutland! And Huntingdonshire. Where's that gone? Who said they could go messing about with counties like that? I was never consulted, was I?'

'But – '

'And now this tunnel business! Everyone says they don't want a tunnel but we're having a tunnel anyway. I mean – you know!'

Sensing that like the railway system, I had run out of steam, Bridget spoke again.

'But you never did anything, Adrian. You've always gone on about politicians being silly and it being a waste of time thinking about that sort of thing. You knew all these things were happening really, you just couldn't be bothered to get involved!'

I get fed up with my wife being right, but she usually is. She was this time.

I suppose my life has tended to be like my weekly trips to the BBC, running along rather cosy ruts of non-involvement.

I think part of my Christian commitment should have been finding ways to express my discontent with loss of quality of life, even – or especially – over questions that have no obvious right answers.

I have not been political, and I repent.

Something Beautiful

I have already confessed that if eavesdropping was a capital offence I would have been hanged years ago. I don't know what the visual equivalent of eavesdropping is, but I'm afraid I have to plead guilty to that as well. I am continually entertained, distracted and absorbed by the things that people are doing in my immediate vicinity. Concentrated observation can function like a mental telescope sometimes, revealing large significance in small events – babies being born in stables, for instance.

Similarly, one of the most delicately beautiful things I ever witnessed was on the platform of Beckenham Junction railway station. An unlikely setting I agree, but that's where it was. Having just recorded a television sermon in a private house in Beckenham at a painfully early hour of the morning, I strolled down to the station to begin my journey home, contemplating as I went the very pleasant prospect of the rest of Saturday stretching ahead with nothing very arduous to be done in it.

It was a grey, overcast morning filled with the damp threat of rain, and I had nearly an hour to wait before my train was due to arrive. I didn't mind. Like Chesterton I have always (well, nearly always) enjoyed being stranded in railway stations. I bought a newspaper, sat on a bench near the ticket barrier, and was soon lost in the sports pages.

My attention was diverted after a few minutes by a clattering noise coming from the inside area where the tickets were sold. The noise stopped for a moment or two, presumably while tickets were being purchased, then it began again, becoming louder and louder, until a young couple appeared at the ticket barrier carrying a large wooden object between them. They lowered it to the ground while the man on the barrier inspected their tickets.

It was a table. I peered inquisitively at it round the side of my newspaper. It certainly wasn't a particularly distinctive piece of furniture – quite nice, but nothing special. One of those old-fashioned circular gate-leg tables, the kind that fold down on both sides, and are supported by carved spiral legs. It wasn't even in especially good condition. There must have been two or three generations' worth of stains and knocks on the bits that I could see. A good sanding and polishing prospect – if you had the time – but nothing special.

The two people were very ordinary looking as well. A young man and a girl, probably no more than twenty years old. I watched them carry their table on to the platform after the ticket inspector had agreed that it could travel on the train with them. He had seemed somewhat flummoxed at first by the fact that it was not a dog or a bicycle.

As the two young people came towards me I studied their faces. She was quite pretty, and they both had pleasant, open expressions. Their eyes declared that they were each enjoying exactly the same level of happiness, a quite reliable indicator that true love is present. They made me want to smile.

The table was lowered gently on to a spot roughly half-way between my bench and the edge of the platform. I folded my newspaper casually and pretended to stare vacantly at the opposite platform.

The girl took some coins out of her pocket, did what appeared to be a rapid calculation, then dashed out of the station again, presumably to buy sweets or a paper at the shop opposite the ticket office.

While she was gone, her friend embarked on a little, light-footed circular stroll around the table, clearly locked into orbit by the sheer pleasure of ownership. It was almost a restrained skip that he was doing. He did *try* to look casual and suitably bored, but he couldn't quite manage it. Every now and then he would stop, move a little closer, just touch the wood gently with the tips of his fingers, and smile a small, private, happy smile before going on to do another revolution.

When the girl returned the couple stood side by side, gazing fondly down at their piece of furniture like parents with a new baby. They stroked its top and pointed out bits of it to each other; they patted it and whispered about it and made arranging movements in the air with their hands, as though they were planning where to put it, all with a restrained delight that lit them both up like lightbulbs.

Unless I was very much mistaken that table was going to be the centrepiece of some newly acquired house or flat or perhaps even a bedsitter – they didn't look very well off. Something made me sigh a little as I imagined them arriving home and setting about the business of sanding and fixing and polishing their prize before finally putting it in different parts of the room to see how it looked.

There was such a glow in and around this little scene, that I stood up and moved a little closer, hoping (at least I'm honest) to overhear what they were actually saying. I think it was more than that, though. I wanted, silly as it sounds, to be nearer to the innocent joy of what was going on.

But, as it happened, their train came in at that moment, and seconds later, they carried their baby very carefully into one of the carriages and slammed the door behind them.

I felt all sorts of things at that moment: sadness, because I'd lost the kind of simplicity that produces the depth of pure appreciation I had just seen; pleasure, because it was just a lovely thing to watch; and a new understanding about what Paul the apostle meant when he encouraged us to look at whatever is beautiful. I could feel how good it was for me.

Perhaps, also, there was something about transfiguration, a word that, very broadly defined, means making things shine because of love.

I don't know if an old table could really shine, but I did have the absurd notion that the platform had become just a little darker as that train disappeared round a distant bend, on its way to the city.

Thou Shalt Not Kick the Cat

A final confession: I am emotionally handicapped in the area of 'conflict'. I don't know how to handle it.

A little while ago I was asked to speak on this subject. It wasn't an area I felt confident about, and I wasn't at all sure where to start. Eventually, after much moaning and growling and head scratching, I decided to go through Mark's gospel and list the occasions on which Jesus came into conflict with people or ideas or anything else. This catalogue of confrontation turned out to be much longer and more significant than I had anticipated. Jesus was in conflict with:

Demons: There was nothing polite about the master's way with these horrible in-dwellers.

Illness: Very early on in the gospel we read of Jesus healing Simon Peter's mother-in-law (much to the disgust of contemporary Jewish Les Dawsons, no doubt) and the leper, who so moved him to pity. Physical affliction was confronted and dismissed.

Weather: Jesus commanded a storm to 'be still'.

Nazarenes: The inhabitants of Jesus' home town were offended by the authority of his teaching and the claims he made. (How often do we fail to 'allow' people we know well to change, and thereby miss out on what God is offering us through them?)

The scribes and Pharisees: What a hard time he gave them! Not just through direct criticism, but also with witty, disconcerting replies to their trick questions. ('By whose authority do you do these things?' and 'Should we pay taxes to Caesar?')

His own disciples: He told them off on a number of occasions, usually when they had arrived at a committee-like decision about what ought to happen next, or what he really meant. At one point, after Jesus had talked of his imminent betrayal, death and resurrection, Mark tells us

114

that the disciples 'didn't understand and were afraid to ask him'. Jesus was clearly determined that his followers were not going to turn his life into religion. (He's just as determined nowadays.)

Peter was admonished particularly strongly when he attempted to deflect Jesus from the dismally unattractive path of obedience. How many of us are doing the same thing in relation to people like Terry Waite? As well as praying for his safe return, should we not also be thanking God that this servant of his is in the right place at the right time, for reasons that we could not hope to understand at this stage?

His own father: At that terrible moment when our sin cut Jesus off from the roots of his own being, he was in sudden panic-stricken conflict with the person he had trusted most.

Because of those words – 'My God, my God, why have you forsaken me?', we can be sure that there is an experience of emptiness and rejection in the heart of God that compassionately echoes and empathises with similar darkness in the hearts of men.

That's only part of the list, and it doesn't include or mention the occasions when, much to his disciples' bewilderment, Jesus chose to avoid or withdraw from conflict when it seemed the most obvious option (the healing of the centurion's ear, for instance). Clearly, conflict is intended to be of positive use in our lives. So why do we see so little of it? What do we do with the legitimate confrontational impulses that spring up in us? I can only answer for myself.

(a) My family gets it in the neck instead of the person or people who should have been faced. This is the familiar 'kicking the cat' syndrome.

(b) I turn it inwards. I'm told that depression is unexpressed anger. Bottled up feelings can have a bad effect spiritually, mentally and physically.

(c) I release my aggression in the form of GOSSIP, one of the most destructive activities for a church community. Anger disguised as concern and passed on to others acts like poison.

'I like John – I really do. That's why it concerns me so much that he's beginning to. . . .'

'In confidence and just for prayer, but have you heard about Jill. . . .'

(d) I sulk. Instead of expressing displeasure or unhappiness openly, I play games, usually of the sort where the person I feel hurt by has to 'guess' that I'm feeling upset.

(e) I dilute the strength of my own convictions through fear of open conflict. This can happen when matters of faith are at issue, or when I ought to complain to the plumber yet again because the central heating *still* isn't working properly. I hear my own voice bleating out compromises when I should be sure and strong.

(f) I am very fortunate in that I am able to conflict with institutions and ideas through writing and speaking, but there are temptations here as well to be either too harsh or too soft.

So what can I do to change things?

First, I learn, through the way Jesus behaved, that there is a middle way of assertiveness between cowardice and outright aggression. Most of us find this approach quite difficult. It involves expressing the way we feel in a calm and clear fashion before we have let things continue for so long that we are only capable of exploding or gossiping or sulking. It will feel risky, because the person we address may not choose to meet us at the place where we wish to meet them. More often, though, I suspect that potentially explosive situations will be defused by such an approach and relationships actually improved. I wonder how many times I have impeded forward movement in my own Christian community by keeping quiet when I should have spoken, or speaking when I should have kept my mouth shut?

Secondly, and most important of all, I need to make sure that I am praying with concentration and urgency for real guidance about when to enter into conflict and when to withdraw. This is not an optional extra, but an essential.

Ultimately, I suppose, we are seeking to demonstrate the simplicity and straightforwardness of children, the sort of children who will not be afraid to say what they think, but will always be ready to receive guidance from wise parents.

Blushes and Bloomers

All right! One more little confession: I do have a certain tendency to get myself into embarrassing situations.

Years ago I was asked to read about the psychology of embarrassment as part of my teacher training course at Stockwell College in Bromley.

Most of the brain cells that collected this information seem to have dropped off since that time, but some of what I learned remains.

As far as I can remember, the theory presented to us was that embarrassment happens when people slip or are forced out of roles appropriate to the situation or environment they are in. This can produce 'role-conflict', which, said the books, is the real basis of the kind of uncomfortable confusion that we call embarrassment.

For example, if I am sitting in a theatre listening to a stand-up comic performing from the stage, role-conflict may easily occur. If the comedian's jokes are funny, and I laugh, then no embarrassment is caused. His role is to amuse, my role is to *be* amused. If, however, his act is so dire that I find myself unable to laugh at his jokes, then I may well squirm with embarrassment in my seat, all too aware that because he has failed in his role as an entertainer I am failing miserably in my role as an audience member. If the rest of the audience are as little amused as I am, then, of course, the performer himself will experience equal or perhaps even more profound embarrassment about the failures of his own role – poor chap.

One of my most memorably embarrassing real-life experiences happened on a single-decker bus travelling from Tunbridge Wells to Heathfield when I was quite a young man. The bus was crowded with shoppers, and I ended up sitting in a window seat, next to a young mother laden with various packages and carrier bags. She looked hot and tired, as young mothers so often do, and she had somehow become separated from her little girl who was sitting in the window seat directly behind me, completely blocked in by one of those enormously fat men who wear very short, tight pullovers.

As we approached a stop at around the half-way point in our journey, my neighbour gathered her assortment of belongings, stood up, and turned round rather worriedly, obviously about to ask the fat man to let her daughter out. Thinking that I could help, I also turned round and put my hands under the little girl's arms, intending to lift her over to her mother. Unfortunately, I misjudged the child's weight rather drastically. She was much lighter than I thought. The result was that I piledrove her into the roof of the bus, so hard that as she came down her eyes were crossed by the power of the impact. As the mother leaned across to rescue her daughter my cheeks burned. It must have looked so horribly deliberate.

Mother and child left the bus, and as we moved away again I glanced over my shoulder. The fat man was gazing reproachfully at me. 'Why', his expression seemed to ask, 'did you just commit that act of gratuitous violence against a poor defenceless little girl?'

Far from seeing me in the role of 'helper' he obviously saw me as a 'batterer'. I was embarrassed. I was *very* embarrassed.

Far more recently, during a family holiday in Europe, I was in trouble again. This time I made an idiot of myself in a cable-car on the way up to the top of Mont Blanc. The car was full of tourists, mainly French-speaking with a smattering of Japanese tourists who uttered very satisfactorily oriental gasps of awe and wonder as the panorama of snow-covered ranges came into view.

A benign, rather stout French lady of advanced years offered my two young sons a sweet each. They, of course, accepted, and it seemed to me an ideal opportunity to demonstrate my profound knowledge of the Gallic tongue.

My wife, sensing from my knitted brows and glazed eyes that I was composing a sentence in French, made frantic attempts to reach me in time to avert disaster, but she was on the other side of the car and didn't make it in time. Tapping the generous French lady on the shoulder I smiled warmly and said something that was supposed to mean 'You are obviously a grandmother yourself'.

The smile disappeared from the old lady's face as though I had slapped her. Grunts and clicks of disapproval emanated from the other French-speakers. I noticed that my wife gazed intently through the window at nothing at all.

'What did I say?' I hissed. 'Was the grammar wrong or something'

'Unfortunately,' said Bridget, from the side of her mouth, 'you sounded quite confident and fluent. That's what made it so awful!'

'Yes, but what did I say?'

It appeared that what I had said to the lady with the sweets was: 'Well, you *are* a large women, aren't you?'

More role confusion – more embarrassment!

The next step of our college education in this area concerned the nature and function of 'tact'. A tactful person, our lecturer told us, is one who restores or repairs roles that have become inappropriate, caused embarrassment or upset relationships.

'Perhaps he was only trying to help. . . . I'm sure he didn't mean it. . . . He might have been trying to help the little girl when he lifted her . . .' – that sort of thing.

The Christian faith is concerned with breakdown in the relationship between God and man. God created men and women to be in a loving relationship with him, and as long as individuals are not fulfilling this most appropriate of roles there will continue to be a sort of cosmic embarrassment.

I don't know if Jesus' death and resurrection can really be described as the ultimate exercise in tact, but it is the only way I know of repairing the damage that occurred somehow, way back in the past, when, as the Bible has it, Adam and Eve, having spoiled their friendship with God, suddenly recognised their own nakedness and were deeply embarrassed.

Performance
Fellowshipping in the Petrol

I used to be even more naïve than I am now. I honestly thought that the only thing a writer really needed was the ability to write. I now know that accountancy skills, legal expertise, a sponge-like readiness to read what my aunt's friend's second cousin has written with a blunt pencil on greaseproof paper, sufficient fortitude to provide the same answers to the same questions over and over again at local radio stations, and enough humble restraint to avoid hunting down adverse reviewers and mugging them in back alleys, are just a few of the extra talents that must be developed. They don't do evening classes in things like Forgiving Reviewers, so most of it has to be self-taught.

Take book-signing for instance. You-know-who's law operates here with a vengeance. If I undertake a speaking engagement and decide not to take any books to sell, invariably, as soon as I finish bleating, I'm descended upon by a howling mob, wolfishly intent on consuming every word I've ever written. Conversely, if, in a fever of confidence, I have large numbers of books delivered by my publishers to a venue, then I'm almost certain to end up staggering miserably on and off trains and buses with huge unwieldy parcels of books at the end of the day. When, by some miracle, supply and demand do happen to coincide, I find it essential to bear in mind one of the few lessons that has sunk in at last. You cannot sign books and take the money for them at the same time. Well – you might be able to, but I certainly can't.

I'm hopeless with money at the best of times. More than one taxi driver, after I've offered a note in payment and asked in magnanimous tones for a particular amount of change, has pointed out dispassionately that I've awarded myself a substantial tip. So, signing books with one hand and giving change with the other is completely beyond me. Not only does my left hand not know what my right hand is doing and vice versa, but my brain loses control over both. My consequent tendency to sign five pound notes and dump paperbacks in the cash tray is viewed with some alarm by the good Christian folk who approach with simple faith in my sanity. Nowadays I ask organisers kindly to provide someone to 'do the money'. This is an immense relief because I really enjoy meeting people and writing in their books – as long as that's all I have to do.

I read somewhere recently that the travelling Christian speaker is likely to face three main temptations. These are, in no particular order, sex, power and money. Well, all I can say is that I must be on the wrong circuit. I'm always on the look-out for opportunities to heroically resist the queue of seductive temptresses that should be waiting outside my hotel door, but so far not one has put in an appearance. I'm not complaining, Lord – honestly!

The desire to wield power over congregations,

readers and audiences is a temptation that is much more likely to come my way, but the fact that God has taken me by the scruff of the neck and said, 'Plass, your role in life is to be a sort of public idiot for me', has removed most of my chances for sinful indulgence in this area. I rather think that my family's jolly little satirical jibes might be a sufficient safeguard in any case, when it comes to taking myself too seriously as a writer or speaker.

As for money, I'd love to be in a position to turn down *most* of some unhealthily large sum, but no one's ever offered me one. On the contrary, a particular problem can arise in this connection, usually at the end of a speaking and signing session.

Many churches and organisations have a healthy and realistic attitude to expenses and fees for visiting speakers or entertainers. Their generosity touches and amazes me sometimes. But there are others, few but memorable, where gloomy treasurers enquire if they might 'have fellowship in the petrol', and it is in these situations that the afore-mentioned problem is likely to crop up. The scene is as follows.

The signing is finished, the people have gone, the evening is over. All that is left is me, my remaining books and the mournful distributor of precisely correct travelling expenses. Frowningly he filters out the appropriate sum from a small leather purse while I count the cash from the book sales. If a lot of books have gone there might be quite a pile of five and ten pound notes, as well as the usual collection of coins. Leaning over the table deep in calculation, I gradually become aware that the filterer is directing a sternly reproachful gaze at the wad of notes in my hand.

'What', his expression seems to ask 'is a Christian doing with all that money? Why?' it seems to enquire further 'are you taking expenses from our ill-provided coffers when you have already through your coarse marketing taken such huge sums from our ill-provided people?'

When I was a raw beginner, this would trigger me into defensive babbling about how much I had to pay for the books, how little profit I made on each one, how hard it was to support a wife and three children when you were freelance and how, as a Christian, money really meant nothing to me. There were times when I came very close to thrusting payment on the treasurer as a thank-offering for inviting me to speak.

I don't do that any more. I ignore gazes. It's another of those things I've had to learn about being a writer: Never answer questions you haven't actually been asked – especially about money.

So much to learn; but I'm getting there slowly. Perhaps if I really work at mastering all these extra skills, I shall be able to set aside a few hours each week to actually do a little writing.

Baptism of Fire

After speaking at the kind of event I've just described, I enjoy meeting people at the coffee and chat session before everyone goes home. During that buzzing half hour or so I've often been asked if I am a speaker who started to write, or a writer who started to speak.

The truth is that the writing came first. *Join the Company*, my initial faltering step into the world of books, was an almost instant worst-seller, but *The Sacred Diary of Adrian Plass*, which had already been appearing as a column in Family Magazine for a year or so, did very much better. As a result, I was invited to do some readings at the big Christian festival known as Spring Harvest. I thought I might be nervous when the time came, but I wasn't – I was terrified.

Shortly after returning from Minehead I recorded my nerve-wracking experience for posterity. I do hope it doesn't discourage potential speakers!

I am booked into Spring Harvest with my wife and three children. I am to read extracts from my *Sacred Diary* on the Fringe shows.

Only about three people have heard of my diary. I am very nervous.

We arrive very late at night. My seven-year-old son, Joseph, is sick just outside the main gate. This does not seem a good omen. Being a Christian, I ignore it. The weather is like that bit in *The Guns of Navarone*, just before they climb the cliff in the blinding rain.

We find the office and collect the key to our chalet. We find our chalet. There is a man n it. He is about as pleased to see us as we are to see him.

We say things like 'Praise the Lord!' and 'Where are you from, brother?' He is to share with us for one night. We are all hearty. Luckily, he is nice.

I am amazed by the chalet. It is new. It has a colour TV. It has a kitchen area. It has nice furniture. We settle in. Joseph is sick again. We go to bed. We sleep.

On Monday I go to a meeting of Spring Harvest staff. There are famous Christians there. We sing choruses. We get into small groups for prayer. There is a famous Christian leading mine. He suggests that we should thank God, one by one, for what he has done for us today.

I am the last to pray. Everyone else seems to have about fifteen things to say thank you for. I say to God in my mind, 'I can't think what to thank you for'. God sighs, and says, 'If only you knew, Plass. If only you knew!' I think of one or two things to say. I try to sound warm and devout. I actually feel rather sweaty and apprehensive.

Clive Calver, General Secretary of the Evangelical Alliance, speaks to us all. He exhorts us. He tells a joke. Everyone is very sympathetic. He tells us to divide into large, activity groups. We do. I am in the entertainment group. I turn to the person next to me and whisper, 'I don't go in for all this "famous Christian" rubbish, do you?' He looks a little disgruntled. I learn later that he is a famous Christian.

Later still, I tell my wife about the meeting. She suggests the reason I go on about famous Christians is that I'm annoyed because I'm not one. What nonsense!

The next evening I am due to do my first reading in the Multi Media Mega Show. I arrive early. I try to look cool. I am absolutely petrified. Soon, several hundred teenagers surge in through the doors with a mighty rushing sound. I gibber a silent prayer. God says, 'I am not a bottle of whisky, Plass'. I reply, 'I wish you were'. I repent hurriedly. God smiles. He can take a joke.

Steve Flashman, an old friend, has started the show. He is the host. He is very good. It is very good. Steve's wife, Sue, is very good. The teenagers enjoy it very much. Oh, heavens! Why should I spoil their pleasure?

Steve is very lively indeed. I consider the fact that he is the same age as I am. I decide that he must play squash or something.

There are videos and competitions and live performances and flashing lights. Suddenly it is my turn! Steve is introducing me. I yearn for sudden illness, natural disaster, the second coming, or anything to rescue me. Nothing does.

I climb up on the stage and look out towards the audience. There seem to be about a million teenagers jamming the auditorium. They are waiting in the dark to find out if I'm funny or not. The back of my throat sticks against the front. My stomach is full of cold, bubbling porridge. A muscle in the calf of my right leg starts to twitch uncontrollably.

I feel certain that I was only ever cut out to be a minor clerk in a huge firm, with no responsibility at all. If none of these two million horrible youngsters laugh, I will die. I ask myself what can have possessed me to believe I could ever stand up and read this appalling rubbish to three million killer-teenagers.

I have already paused for nearly four seconds since my quota of encouraging applause. If I do not start soon they will think I am a loony. I am a loony. Why else am I volunteering to destroy my self-image in front of four million people, all at a most unattractive age?

I begin. My voice clambers with an effort from between my tonsils. The first few words land like slabs of dough on the stage in front of me. Then, a wonderful, wonderful person near the back laughs loudly. Another person laughs. Several people laugh. Nearly everybody is laughing. Of course, I say to myself, I always knew I could trust teenagers. They are insightful people. A very attractive age group. As I complete the reading, I mentally resign from the minor clerkship and rehearse the expression of pleased but humble surprise that I shall adopt when confronted by the host of *This is Your Life* at some future date.

The applause is loud enough and prolonged enough to provoke me into performing a series of complicated spiritual gymnastics in order to remain humble. I fail. I climb down from the stage. My knees have turned to jelly. My stomach has turned to jelly. My brain has turned to jelly.

When the show is over, some of the teenagers come up to my wife and me. They say they thought my bit was good. I am pleased. One of the girls says to Bridget, 'It must be a real laugh living with him'. Bridget snorts. She says, 'Oh yes, it's a real laugh living with him, especially first thing in the morning.' I cough and suggest it's time we went. We go back to our chalet.

The week goes on.

Our children disappear every morning to their club. One is an 'ant', the other is an 'elephant'. Bridget and I miss them very much. That is not true.

We go to a talk by Winkie Pratney. He makes us laugh. We go to a talk by Lyndon Bowring. He makes us cry. We go to a talk by Eric Delve. He makes us laugh and cry, despite the fact that we have heard this one before in Luton. We go to a talk by Clive Calver. He makes us write a letter. We hear Chris Bowater sing. We are entranced.

We take an afternoon off and climb the hill behind Minehead to the place where Exmoor starts. We play a game among the trees with the children. It is as enchanted a place as any that A. A. Milne knew. Far below, the sea stretches away into the distance for ever. I ask God if this is a place where souls can be repaired. He says, 'Don't be sentimental, Plass. Just enjoy it.' I do.

I go to the New International Variety Show. It is hosted by Stuart Penny. I am to read a further extract from my diary later on. First, Stuart Penny holds a corny joke competition. The winner is the one who tells the corniest joke. A small girl enters. She comes up on the stage.

Everybody thinks she is sweet. They say, 'Aaah, isn't she sweet?' He holds the microphone close to the little girl's mouth.

She says, 'Why did the Romans build long straight roads?' Stuart Penny has not heard this joke before. If he had he would have pushed the sweet little girl off the stage at this point. Instead, he turns his head and smiles at the audience as if to say, 'Isn't she sweet?' He turns back to the little girl and says, 'Why did the Romans build long straight roads?' She replies, in a loud, clear voice, 'So the Pakis couldn't build corner shops'.

All the good Christians look concerned. All the others can't help laughing at the situation. I am one of the others. I laugh. Stuart Penny doesn't know whether to laugh or cry.

Somewhere in the audience the little girl's mummy and daddy are trying to cut their throats with the edge of their meter cards.

It is time to read my diary. I read some. I lose my place at a crucial point. The audience laughs far more at me losing my place than at anything I have actually read. I do not resent this. I forgive them. It is lucky there is not a machine gun handy.

I go into a Celebration one evening. I sit at the back. I look around. There are a lot of men with short, neat hair and hopeful expressions. There are quite a lot of beards. I have a beard. Most of the women look as if they have suffered more than the men.

I say to God, 'Is this your army, God?'

God says, 'I don't know if they're an army, but they're certainly mine. Why?'

I say, 'They're a bit odd aren't they?'

God says, 'You're a bit odd, Plass, but I put up with you, don't I? If *I* love them, then you'd better. All right?'

I say, 'All right, God, I'll try'.

Spring Harvest is going to sleep as I walk back through the darkness afterwards. I feel peaceful for once.

Heaven's Heroes

That first visit to Spring Harvest was very important to me. It was the beginning of a completely different way of life, and I shall never forget the pungent emotions of excitement and fear that accompanied my early experiences of entertaining and speaking. Over the year that followed I became quite insufferably fond of the sound of my own voice, until, having exhausted the novelty of 'being known', I settled down a little into the business of attempting to communicate for a living. In the process I began to learn (and am still learning) that unless my writing and speaking is rooted in real relationship with God and Man, there simply isn't anything to communicate. I have also begun to learn how passionately concerned God is with people, things and situations that may be small and insignificant in the eyes of the world, and even, at times, the Church.

Last year, for instance, four years on from my first encounter with 'killer teenagers', I was once more working for Spring Harvest at Minehead and Skegness (not simultaneously), and there were new lessons to learn in this respect.

Spring Harvest itself has not changed a great deal. It was the same big Christian knees-up, bringing together thousands from all denominations to enjoy teaching, worship and holiday-making. As usual, the thing I enjoyed most about this annual extravaganza was meeting old friends, making new ones and drinking free coffee in the team lounge. One of the friends I renewed acquaintanceship with was Andy Butcher, erstwhile editor of the monthly magazine *Christian Family*, now seeing his spirituality cubed daily as he worked for YOUTH WITH A MISSION in Holland. That was a pleasant re-union. It was Andy who suggested *The Sacred Diary of Adrian Plass*, a monthly column that later became a book which radically altered the direction of my life.

Spring Harvest, 1990, was even bigger and more dramatic than ever, especially during the Big Top worship, where huge numbers gathered each day.

For me, however, this particular year was marked by three rather undramatic events, the first of which happened before I even got there.

The evening before our departure I went to a meeting in my own church, St Mary's Hailsham, at about 7.30 p.m. By the time I came out at 9.45 the rain was bucketing down.

I had neither coat nor umbrella. Then Topsy offered me a lift in her taxi.

Topsy is an elderly and much loved member of our church who goes to just about every meeting throughout the week – despite the fact that she can only get around with some difficulty nowadays.

She took my arm and we moved very slowly along the church path and towards the taxi that was waiting a hundred yards away. My best suit was getting soaked – and so was I.

I could have done that distance in fifteen seconds flat. But then – I don't know what you think about God talking to people – I began to laugh because I could sense him saying to me, 'Hard luck, Plass, this is the pinnacle of your Christian achievement. You will probably never do anything much more important than this – including your bleating at Spring Harvest.'

The second thing happened the next day when I arrived at Butlin's, Minehead. I met a girl called Anita Hydes who was also working at the festival, but as a 'detached youth worker' – one of the most difficult and demanding tasks on site.

I'd met Anita very briefly before, and I knew she was the subject of a book called *Snatched From the Flames* but I'd never really had a chance to chat with her.

Anita is an attractive character, with a smile that lights up her face, but I have rarely met anyone in whom the marks of past grief and agonies are so evident.

Abused, beaten up and raped as a child, she went on to heroin at the age of fifteen and was an addict for seventeen years.

She was imprisoned for supplying drugs on more than one occasion, and was continually involved in acts of violence – often against the police.

At the end of the 70s she was admitted to hospital suffering from septicaemia and given three days to live.

Rescued and taken home by a friend who happened to be an ex-addict and a Christian, Anita spent the next three years recovering from the effects of drugs. During that time she made a Christian commitment herself.

Today Anita is a YMCA coffee-bar worker as well as being a regular prison visitor – especially concerned for those going through the same things as she did.

Much of her time is also spent replying to letters from people who've read about her and need help or advice themselves.

I spend quite a lot of time knocking the Church on a professional basis – but I don't knock God for what he's done with Anita. Hers is an amazing story.

The third event was so slight as to be hardly noticeable.

After two or three days at Minehead I met a teenage girl who described to me what happened after she read *The Lion, The Witch and The Wardrobe*, C. S. Lewis' book about a group of children who discover a different world through the back of an old wardrobe.

She was quite a little girl at the time, and very excited about the story.

Without telling anyone what she was doing, she climbed into the bottom of her parents' wardrobe, closed the door, and sat in the dark for an hour, waiting for the magic to start.

That simple little anecdote touched me very deeply. How many other people at that huge Christian get-together – children and adults – had been sitting in the bottom of their metaphorical wardrobes, waiting for the magic to start?

Topsy, Anita and the child at the bottom of the wardrobe – three people who reminded me that God's concern is for those individuals who may not be important in the world's eyes.

Not a bad thing to remember in a Christian world that still demands its heroes.

A Voice from the Past

You can never tell when or how God is going to teach you a lesson. It happened to me once when I was away speaking in Reading at the Greyfriars Centre in Friar Street. I was due to start my customary bleating at about eight-fifteen, but first I spent a very pleasant couple of hours at the home of John Brown, the centre manager.

John is a bluff, genial Northerner with a tough core, and a genuine determination to communicate Jesus in the real world. He also has a charming wife, Margaret, who I'm sure keeps him going with great love and expertise through the tough times; not to mention four very interesting children who are surprisingly clear about their projected careers. As far as I can remember, the

Brown household is scheduled to produce a Prime Minister, a chiropracter, a soldier and an American footballer.

It was the American Footballer's seventh birthday party on the day when I was there; great bumps and crashes from upstairs bore witness to the fact that Steve had 'a few friends round'. I met them a little later, when they war-whooped their way down to consume vast quantities of chocolate biscuits and sausage rolls and little sandwiches.

Later still, I ate an excellent supper with the political, medical and military elements of the family – known commonly as Rachel, Emma (she with designer holes in her jeans), and Tim, who had supervised most of the bumps and crashes.

Altogether it was an unusually relaxing prelude to the kind of evening event that had punctuated my life with increasing frequency over the preceding year. As we drove from John's house to the centre, I realised that I was getting a bit jaded generally. Trying to fit too many different things in, perhaps.

Like the Christian greengrocer or the Christian brain surgeon, however, I knew that the job had to be done, however I felt. It was nice to have started with the experience of being an honorary Brown, though.

I began my talk that evening as I often do, by speaking about how I was converted at the age of sixteen after hearing a sermon about the thief on the cross, preached by a man called Denis Shepherd who had served in the Merchant Navy before training for ordination into the Anglican Ministry.

I was a very awkward, unhappy teenager at the time, unsure about my own identity and generally mistrustful of others. Over the years I had cobbled together a personality of sorts, but it was a façade, and a thin one at that. Chaos reigned within, making me as vulnerable as many teenagers were in the sixties, to the wide variety of cut-price philosophies, religions and negative subcultures that abounded in towns like Tunbridge Wells, where I lived. Drugs, scientology, obscure eastern religions summarised in paperback, weekend violence and sexual experimentation were among the options open to young people like me.

I started going to an after-church youth meeting because there were girls there. I was interested in girls. Eventually the resident curate impressed me deeply with the sheer passion of his feelings about Jesus, and, in an attempt to track down the root or source of this passion, I began to attend the evening service at St John's church, always sitting at the back and always resisting the temptation to get too involved.

Then came Denis Shepherd's sermon. He talked about how one of the thieves who was crucified next to Jesus turned and saw in the face of this strange man a totally unexpected possibility of 'happy ever after'.

'Will you remember me when you come into your kingdom?' he asked.

The thing that impressed me was that Jesus didn't reply that it depended on his spirituality, or his theology, or his quiet-time, or his denomination, or his knowledge of the Bible, or how good he was able to be in the short time left to him; he simply said 'Yes', and promised that they would be together in heaven that very day.

After the service I prayed a very simple prayer with the preacher, and my relationship with Jesus began on that day. Much storm and calm was to follow over the years, but that was the beginning and it was very important to me.

I went on to tell the folk at Greyfriars about subsequent problems, and to attempt to identify the kind of 'rubbish' that had obscured the truth about Jesus for so many years of my life. It was three quarters of an hour later, when I was about to get going again after a short break, that something unexpected happened.

John Brown, no lightweight himself, ascended the platform and announced that he wanted to say a few words. He asked me if I'd ever seen *This Is Your Life* on television. My heart sank for a moment. Set up!

I imagined a succession of people from my past coming in through the side door and saying things like: 'Calls himself a Christian, eh? I can tell you a thing or two. . . .' I measured John Brown for a left-hook, followed by a flying drop kick, perhaps.

'Do you recognise this voice?' he asked. A tape-recording began to play through the loud-speakers. It was Denis Shepherd, the man who had preached that sermon nearly twenty-five years ago at St John's Church in Tunbridge Wells.

His message was one of greeting and encouragement. I was quite stunned! When the recording finished, John explained that Denis is a member of Greyfriars Church, working full-time as an evangelist for the Church Pastoral Aid Society. He was away for my visit, but had left a taped message to be played during the evening.

I felt quite shaken as I stood up to continue my talk. Later, as I sat in the passenger seat of a friend's car, speeding through the darkness towards Hailsham and home, it occurred to me that I'd been reminded of the two most important things in my life.

First, the Brown family brought my own houseful to mind. I knew that I would never be entrusted with a more important ministry than the one towards my wife and four children.

Secondly, the voice of Denis Shepherd had brought back that day, so long ago, when I met and loved Jesus for the first time.

Those were the really important things, and I would always be jaded if I was neglecting such essential priorities.

Failing Frankly

One of the questions that I faced when I began speaking publicly to Christian groups was the one about honesty. Just how truthful is it possible to be in a context where, traditionally, the chap up at the front is as near to a shining example as you are likely to get? Unrelenting frankness can have a curious effect on Christian groups, who expect their visiting speakers to fall into one of a limited number of familiar categories.

I spoke once in a jam-packed sitting-room to a band of local church members who were very mixed in terms of age and churchmanship. At the end of a lengthy session in which I described my own weaknesses quite graphically, I overheard a brief interchange between a mother and her ten-year-old son at the side of the room.

'Well,' said Mum, 'what did you think of him?'

After a short ponder, the boy replied.

'He was quite nice really – not like a Christian at all.'

I'm quite sure the lad was *not* saying that all the speakers he'd heard before were less than nice, rather that the way I spoke and the things I spoke about failed to match any model he had known previously.

Certainly, from the earliest days of my own Christian experience, I noticed – and still notice – that many preachers and 'professional Christians' appear to have only experienced problems in the past. By the time they stand up in the pulpit or behind the microphone everything is sorted out, tidied up and summarised in nineteen shiny points for the benefit of those who are still struggling. This can be quite intimidating for people like me, who are constantly grappling with an unruly queue of worries, bad habits, weaknesses and poultice-like responsibilities. Guidance and wisdom I certainly need from others to deal with these things, but it's much easier to accept help from one who travels with you, than from one who stands on a distant mountain-top offering detached advice from a great height.

Yes, platform immunity is a very wonderful thing. I know how it happens, though. There's something about standing up in front of a church full of Christians that seems to demand that your spirituality be cubed.

Present miseries and perplexities don't feel like a very good advert for God, whereas a comfortably retrospective look at difficulties overcome gives you, the speaker, a pleasant glow and persuades the listener – quite erroneously, really – that you are engagingly vulnerable and frank.

Often, as I sit down to write a magazine article, or prepare a talk, I feel shredded inwardly. Domestic conflicts over the previous twenty-four hours may have left me feeling wrung-out, inadequate and spiritually blob-like. Is it right on such occasions for me to share those negative experiences with the reader or listener? Some people think not.

A leading evangelical, writing in a magazine produced not a million miles away from the one that I contribute to, recently expressed the view that a current tendency to highlight the difficulties we all share in our Christian lives is not necessarily desirable or helpful. The Bible promises victory and that is what we should be preaching.

Well, I understand that point of view, and I'm all for preachers and writers who map out the route to victory in a practical, helpful and loving way, but – to change the metaphor with a screech of grammatical gears – I can also see the point of occasional dirty linen exhibitions.

Most of the Christians I know well – I would say all, but there may be some paragon I've forgotten – make mistakes, get things wrong, commit sins, get forgiven, get confused, read the Bible, stop reading the Bible, pray, don't pray, feel joyful, feel dismal, experience heaven and plunge into despair.

Being a Christian is a tough, gutsy business, shot through, for me anyway, by the radiance of truth. It seems sad to me that people often feel when they hit a low point that their testimony must be frozen until they have thawed out into a warmer moral or spiritual state.

The analogy of a hospital ward was once suggested to me.

As I enter this hypothetical ward I encounter, in the bed by the door, a patient who is completely encased in bandages from head to foot. Clearly he has suffered some appalling accident and has just been admitted.

He manages to convey to me through the slit left for his mouth that he knows next to nothing about the hospital or the doctor. He's just glad to be there.

A little further up the ward I meet another patient. This person is also very ill, but beginning to recover. He speaks warmly about the treatment he has received, and especially about the doctor who has tended him.

'The ones who've been here a long time tell me he's great,' he says, 'and I'm beginning to realise they're right.'

Towards the far end of the ward a bright-eyed, healthy-looking man is sitting up in bed. He smiles happily, and speaks rapturously about the doctor in charge.

'He's wonderful!' he enthuses. 'I'm completely well!'

In the last bed of all lies a bandage-covered figure just like the one in the first bed. I lean forward to hear what he has to say.

'It's my fifth time', he whispers. 'I keep having these blooming accidents! All my own fault really, but the doc's marvellous. Gets me back on my feet every time. Good job it ain't private!'

It would be very odd if the man in the first bed were to enthuse like the cured man in the third bed.

It would be equally odd if the man in the final bed were not to enthuse about the doctor who has brought him back to health so many times.

And perhaps that's the point really. We are not required to testify to us but to Jesus. If we are spiritually bright-eyed and bushy-tailed at the time, our words will ring with life and light. But if we feel as I sometimes feel, we shall simply say, in a small but hopeful voice, that he has pulled us out before and he'll pull us out again.

The truth is a powerful testimony.

Ministry and Mistaken Identity

A curious and almost undetectable process has occurred in certain sections of the Church, whereby words and expressions have become cloaks for human failure or self-delusion.

Take for example those occasions when church-based drama presentations or outreach evenings attract only a tiny fraction of the numbers hoped for.

'Well,' someone will say with a knowing smile, 'the Lord will have brought the ones he wanted to be here.'

Loosely translated this means either that the advertising was far from adequate, the whole concept was ill-judged, or that local folk are all too well acquainted with the usual standard of productions.

There's nothing deliberate or sinister about this kind of double-think. It's just that a sort of code has been developed to protect us from facing our own inadequacies.

Another, and perhaps even more common, example is the word 'ministry'. Some time ago a man phoned me to make certain money-making suggestions. He seemed to be some variety of Christian entrepreneur. His offers were wildly extravagant.

'After all,' he said, 'you can always use some extra money for your ministry, can't you?'

'My ministry?' I queried. 'What is my ministry?'

'Well – your ministry, you know.'

'But', I said, 'my main ministry is my family.'

'Yeah, quite!' he replied. 'Ministry – family, call it what you like. You can always use some extra cash, right?'

Personally, I think that selling cabbages can involve as valid a ministry as preaching to thousands, but the whole concept has become rather distorted.

The following verses are an attempt to sum up the problems in this area faced by those of us who habitually stand up in front of Christian audiences – I mean congregations.

I want to have a ministry.
I want to be profound,
I want to see the folks I touch
Go spinning to the ground.
I want to use a funny voice,
Mysterious and low,
I want to spot uneven legs,
I want to watch them grow.

I want to have a little team,
No more than two or three,
A totally devoted group
Whose ministry is – me!
They'd keep an eye upon my soul
And tell me how it looks,

And even more importantly
They'd sell my tapes and books.

I want to send my prayer list out,
The printed sort look flash,
The ones that say, 'I'm greatly blessed!
And could you send some cash?'
I'd send them out by first-class post,
And please the folk who got 'em,
By putting little written bits
In biro on the bottom.

I want to be a humble star
At national church events,
And lead obscure seminars
In great big leaky tents.
I want to say how I deplore
the famous Christian hunters,
I want to sign their Bibles
And refer to them as 'punters'.

I really want a ministry
I want to alter lives,
I want to pray for something dead
And see if it revives.
I do! I want a ministry,
I'm sure it's all been planned.
I'll make a start as soon as God,
Removes the job in hand.

The Christian world is still a very small pond in
which musicians, speakers and entertainers can
become very big fish, as long as they don't make

the mistake of swimming out into the huge secular ocean, where a whale can become a sprat in the twinkling of an eye. Very few people who begin as 'names' in the Christian arena make that transition successfully, and there are inbuilt dangers in the very concept of the 'famous Christian', both for the individuals concerned, and for those who provide an audience or congregation for them.

One of my most excruciating memories concerns an incident that occurred at a large Christian festival down towards the west of England. A worship meeting was about to begin, with a thousand or more people present. The leader of the meeting, a very enthusiastic gentleman, came to the microphone, made a couple of practical comments, then produced the following speech.

'I just want to point out to you, folks, that if you look over here' – he pointed – 'you'll see two people you all know well' – he named two famous Christians – 'and I just want to say how great I think it is that they're sitting down there among you all as if they were just ordinary people. Let's give them a round of applause . . .'!

I feel sure that those two people felt as bad as I would have done if I had been applauded for mixing with 'ordinary' people. We know there are *only* ordinary people in the Kingdom of God, but the idea still persists that some have made it farther than others, and are therefore significant in some way.

A couple of years ago I travelled many miles north on a train to speak at a large, modern anglican church. Several people were to be involved in the evening presentation, but it so happened that I reached the venue in the early afternoon, before anyone else arrived. There are few things more desolate than a deserted church complex on a grey afternoon. I trailed dismally around blank brick walls, hunting for an unlocked door.

At last, almost at the point where my circuit had begun, I located a door that squeaked open when I turned the handle and pushed, only to find myself in a small corridor with a door on each side. Putting down my trusty blue suitcase I considered for a moment. Which one should I try?

The clacking of a typewriter from my left decided me. Pushing open the swing door I peered into a room which looked as if it must be the church office. From behind a desk by the window a lady inspected me severely as she suspended her typing operations and removed her glasses. Behind her, on the wall, hung a poster advertising the event that was due to begin in a few hours' time. It featured a rather crude depiction of my face in cartoon form. I loathe pictures of me.

'Yes?' said the typist, her tone as sharp as a hatpin.

'Oh, well,' I foundered, 'I've come to – that is I'm part of the er . . . I'm involved in this evening's thing . . .'.'

'You're very early! We weren't expecting anyone until at least four o'clock.'

'Yes, I know', I writhed, 'I'm very sorry but my train just sort of got here, and er . . . here I am. I wonder if there's a room where I could just wait and . . . well wait?'

'Through the door on the other side of the corridor,' snapped the lady, gesturing dismissively with one hand and replacing her spectacles with the other. 'I believe that's the room they've allocated.'

The clacking began again. Clearly my audience was at an end. I withdrew, taking care not to let the door slam shut. After all, I didn't want my hand smacked.

At least she hadn't recognised me.

When I first began writing and speaking I experienced a pathetically intense thrill every time somebody approached me with the words, 'Aren't you . . .?'

As time has passed, however, the disadvantages of being recognised have become more and more apparent. When you are screaming irrationally at your child outside a tent or chalet at some Christian event, the last thing you want is someone coming up and saying 'Aren't you? . . .?' Besides which, my voice always goes into a sort of bleating neutral whenever I'm asked about my books or anything else connected with the work I do.

What happened half an hour after being sent to my 'allocated' room, though, was much harder to accept. I had just begun to doze happily on the teak edifice that supported me, when there was a gentle tap on the door and my secretarial friend entered with a quite different, coyly apologetic expression on her face. She must, I decided, have caught sight of that poster on the wall behind her desk.

'I'm awfully sorry', she said, continuing with the immortal words: 'I didn't realise who you were.'

Members of the small, loyal band who have grappled with my prose on a number of occasions will be aware that I suffer from the disease of politeness. On this occasion I overcame it.

'Actually,' I said, 'I'm exactly the same person that I was when we met the first time.'

Of course, I know what she meant, and I've done it myself, but what an easy trap it is to fall into. We pay lip-service continually to the principle that there are *no* unimportant people in the eyes of God, and that therefore we must consider all men and women equal; but how difficult it is in practice in the context of ordinary day-to-day interaction. Trained by our upbringing to make judgements according to the criteria of men, we are blinded to the starring role that every individual occupies in the family of God. There are no 'stage extras'.

Mother Teresa says that she sees Christ in every sick or starving beggar that she and her sisters try to help. I hope I can learn from her. I would hate it if, at the end of my life, I looked into the face of Jesus, recognised some humble soul whom I had dismissed as unimportant, and was forced to say, 'I'm awfully sorry, I didn't realise who you were . . .'.'

Television
Who Wrote the Script?

Some time ago I was watching one of our popular soaps. Which one? Well, here are two clues. First, the series is antipodean in origin. That hardly narrows it down at all.

Second, if you say it with an Australian accent it almost rhymes with 'rabies'. Got it? Good.

So, halfway through this particular programme, one of the characters – a girl with long blonde hair and rather simple eyes – gazed almost directly into the camera and said in a voice that throbbed with prefabricated passion. 'I don't understand what's happening to me. I'm not the same any more. Why have I changed?'

'Because, sweetheart', I replied, lounging back intelligently on the sofa with a diet-Pepsi in one hand and a fresh cream doughnut in the other, 'the scriptwriters have ordained that it should be so.

'You are trapped in a soap, and soap washes away all the grey areas. Trauma triumphs! Your destiny is not your own.'

My wife came in just then and asked me – in the sort of tone you use when you don't want to alarm someone who is on the edge of lunacy – why I was talking to the television.

My explanation, which grew quite complex as I warmed to my theme, went something like this:

Just imagine the strange and terrible world of the soap character. Grott and Scarlene, two of the main protagonists in this particular series, have been happily, faithfully married for a score of episodes.

Now, in the shadowy hinterland that such characters must inhabit between the sequences in which they are allowed actually to exist, they hold each other like frightened children, full of a nameless dread.

Scarlene grips a tear-stained script in one white-knuckled hand.

'They're making me fall in love with another man in the next episode!' she sobs. 'Oh Grott, I can't stand it. It turns out that I've been shallow and heartless all along!'

'What!' cries Grott, pulling her even more closely to him, 'despite that scene at Diphne's deathbed when the dialogue clearly established you as a person of deep integrity and warm compassionate maturity?'

'Yes, Grott, I'm nothing but a cheap little trollop!'

An alarming thought strikes Grott. 'What about me, Scarlene? How do I react?'

She clutches the crumpled script yet more firmly. 'Don't make me tell you, Grott!' she pleads.

'Tell me Scarlene! I'd rather you told me.'

She drops her head and speaks in a tense, barely contained whisper. 'You're depressed for three episodes, and then you face up to the fact that you're gay, and fall in love with my brother, Harry.'

'Gay!' screams Grott. 'What about all that suggestive winking and smiling they made us do every time we said goodnight? How can I be gay?'

'You've always been gay without realising it,' explains Scarlene, 'and my betrayal finally reveals what, deep down, you've always known. Oh, Grott, let's run away, somewhere where they can't make us do or be anything!'

'We can't Scarlene,' says Grott sadly, lifting her face to his for a final kiss, 'we're soap characters – we don't really exist. Oh Scarlene . . .'!'

'Oh Grott . . .'!'

'I can't stand here listening to your nonsense all day', interrupted my wife with her usual reverential regard for my ideas. 'I've got things to do.'

'Yes, but the point is . . .''

She'd gone.

The point I was going to make, if you don't mind me telling you instead of her, was that a sudden chill passed through me as I thought about the silly scene I'd just described.

It rang bells somewhere. The idea of living like a puppet, with some other powerful outsider pulling the strings, writing the script, making me do things that were foolish or wrong even when I didn't want to – pre-Jesus bells. And they still tinkle a little nowadays, but nowhere near as loud.

The alarming thing is that a lot of us, including me at times, would rather be in that helpless, driven situation, despite the subtle, underlying

157

horror of it all. Is this because the fear of freedom and responsible choice is even greater? Perhaps more people would be attracted to a robotic Christianity that simply changed the programming, as it were, and marched us into heaven by remote control. Why should freedom be feared?

When I was working with children in care I encountered this problem fairly frequently. It caused great frustration among careworkers who were doing their utmost to help their charges. Many children who had endured appallingly traumatic early lives, followed by a long period of institutional residential placement, were passionately anxious to find foster parents who would offer the kind of loving, relaxed environment that they needed. Care-worker and child would take great trouble over preparation for such a move, including the compiling of a life-history, preparatory visits from and to prospective foster parents, and all the discussion and counselling that were so necessary to the process.

It was very difficult for care-workers (especially the inexperienced ones) to understand why so many children seemed to set out deliberately to sabotage the very thing they wanted so much, often at the point when they were just about to achieve it. One of the boys tried to explain it to me once.

'It's not that you don't want it to happen,' he said, 'and it's not that you don't feel excited and grateful and all that – it's just that you suddenly get frightened, and you think you're going to mess it up anyway, like everything else has always got messed up, so you just make it happen early.'

'But what is it that makes you so frightened?' I asked.

'Being in a family,' he said, 'not knowing what you do or say. Not knowing if they'll just pretend they like you or whether they really will. Besides,' he added, 'it's easier being in a home with all the other kids and staff and that. . . .'

Like many of those who yearn to be part of God's family, he was unable to take a gamble on the reality of love. Better the spiritual half-life of familiar day-to-day existence, than risky meetings with a God who might not turn out to be as loving or forgiving or understanding as his publicity suggests.

You only find out the truth by trying, and it's a terrible fate to be cast for ever in the devil's soap opera. I'm glad I got out when I did.

The Secret of the West Wing

I enjoy a lot of television programmes, but the news frightens me sometimes. The old cliché about good news being no news at all is almost one hundred per cent accurate. Occasionally a quaint or amusing anecdote will be tacked on at the end of a catalogue of woe (if a minute or so has to be filled in), but most of the information we are given is alarming or depressing. All the worst things happening in the world at any given time are condensed into periods of ten to thirty minutes on television. My children are growing up

lopsided awareness of death and disaster.
 move around a quiet Sussex market town
with the threat of Middle East war rumbling
through their heads. They walk to school with
echoes of rape and murder reverberating
through the space behind consciousness. The
reality of mob violence trails them like a trouble-
maker through crowded streets. They have
heard of it all, but experienced none of it. I don't
want them to be totally unaware of all these
things, but I think their view of the world could be
more balanced.

My own reaction to these real-life horror stories is more complex, and perhaps even more
disturbing. Killing in Northern Ireland, brutal
soccer violence, a woman murdered after breaking down on the motorway, someone thrown to
his death in front of a moving lorry after a trivial
argument; grotesque events of this kind provoke
a response in me that contains, not only outrage,
indignation and all the other common reactions,
but also, and rather frighteningly, a sort of echo.

One evening, after a nauseatingly brutal and
brutalised looking football hooligan had grunted
something aggressively into the television camera, I turned to my wife and said, 'They should
drop him down a manhole and weld the lid back
on!'

Even as I spoke, I realised that this absurd
Colonel Blimp-like response was just another
part of my strategy for covering up a deep, cold
fear that is permanently lodged in my innards. I
don't think it's so much a fear of violence directed

towards me (although I'm no keener on being bashed with lead piping than the next man), but rather, a dread of facing the violent impulses that exist *in* me and, I suspect, most other people as well. I am reluctant to face my own creeping awareness that something dark and dangerous is, increasingly, breaking through the shell of what we call civilised behaviour, particularly as my personal definition of civilisation is 'an agreement to pretend that we are not uncivilised'.

I feel sure I am not alone in believing that current types of legislation and policing can no longer contain these symptoms of wildness effectively enough to reassure me. The darkness is not in some conveniently distant sub-group. It exists potentially in all of us, and, in accordance with a cycle that human societies have never successfully broken, it is beginning to affect life in this country to a worrying extent.

Perhaps if we ignore it, it will simply disappear?

As a teenager I rather unwisely read several collections of what were described as 'horror stories'. I was almost addicted to them at one stage, especially the gothic Victorian tales, full of lamplit doom and despair. A theme that occurred more than once in these sombre narratives was that of the lunatic elder son, locked away in a secluded tower room at the far end of the West Wing by his embarrassed or protective family, fed and watered by some ancient family retainer, and much given to howling at midnight when some unsuspecting guest was attempting to sleep.

Those families would have faced terrible problems if a bored and, perhaps, unhappy member of the household had decided that a lunatic on the rampage was far more exciting than the monotony and restrictions imposed upon him by the rest of the family. If he knew where the key to the tower room was kept, and he used it, all hell might be let loose . . . .

The dark and dangerous secret will not just go away, and of course we have to deal with its manifestations on a practical level. I am the first to applaud genuine attempts to look for short-term solutions that will improve political and social structures, and thereby the moral health of our community.

There is no doubt in my mind that the police must continue to do what they do, as well as it can be done. Chaos is not an attractive prospect. Perhaps changes in the social and political climate *will* motivate more socially acceptable activities than soccer violence and other kinds of crude assault. Maybe vigorous efforts by public bodies will help. I hope so.

But I also remember G. K. Chesterton's comment that wife-beating is not 'the poker problem', just as soccer violence is not just a 'drink problem', and addiction is not just a 'drug problem'. They are all People Problems, and they are present, if only in embryonic form, in all of us.

Real individual change demands that we face the dark, secret place in our own personalities with courage and determination. It demands that we invite and experience personal revolution, death and resurrection on the deepest level. The shameful secret of the West Wing must be finally dealt with.

This kind of spiritual transformation is necessary for all of us, however virtuous we feel, or however mild our natures might seem, because the dark pool from which our sin is drawn finds the same level in the whole of mankind. Only the death and resurrection of Jesus happening daily and repeatedly in our lives can drain that pool and keep us clean.

We also need the kind of change that Jesus brings because it is the only type of transformation that has a real chance of surviving the decay of comfortable structures, and the frightening emergence of what we old-fashioned Christians might call 'Original Sin'.

Animals
A Single Sparrow

I've never been quite sure what to think about zoos. I have friends who put forward comprehensive and highly convincing arguments for the abolition of any kind of animal incarceration. Having listened to what they have to say I am amazed that anyone should even remotely consider it right to put wild creatures on display in this way.

'Yes!' I exclaim, 'Yes of course! You're absolutely right! How could I have ever thought otherwise?'

Unfortunately I have another friend, a zoologist, who speaks with equal passion and clarity about the *essential* role played by zoos in the

164

protection and preservation of rare and endangered species. He also is totally convincing.

'How blind I have been!' I cry, when he explains his views to me. 'Thank you for opening my eyes to the truth – you are unquestionably correct in what you say. . . .'

Being in the rather curious position of believing that zoos should be both abolished *and* supported, and believing both things with passionate intensity, does not make it any easier to talk to my children on the subject. Consequently, when they wanted to see some 'wild animals' a couple of summers ago, we compromised and went to a safari park. In the end we got quite excited at the prospect.

We had to spend the equivalent of a month's mortgage repayment to get the six of us in, but we did it. Bridget and I were particularly keen on the big cats. Like thousands of others we wanted the thrills without the teeth.

Our monkeys, on the other hand, wanted to see their monkeys, and none of us were disappointed. Travelling through the animal enclosures in our antediluvian green box on wheels was an odd experience, rather like watching a wild-life programme from inside the television.

The lords of the jungle were impressive but not very lively slabs of lion, laid out in the sunshine, hardly twitching as the endless line of traffic wound slowly past them. Bored and superior, they completely ignored this ever-present phenomenon which experience had shown to be both harmless and invulnerable, unless someone was foolish enough to leave a car, or do something equally rash.

The monkeys were much more active. There was a sign at the entrance to the compound warning drivers that these nimble-fingered little creatures particularly enjoyed 'picking bits' off cars. We could proceed at our own risk.

The warnings were justified. Just in front of us a very smart nearly-new car was covered with the chattering vandals as they pulled out and removed the rubber strip running around the roof rim.

Billowing waves of seething monkey-hate emanated from the helpless car owner, who was prevented from accelerating by the vehicle in front of him. Our car, from which anything removable dropped off long ago, was clearly not an aristocrat amongst monkey targets.

One elderly, half-witted animal clambered laboriously up on to the back of our green box, and sat chewing dismally on little bits of rust before dropping off to confess to his equally ancient mate that he'd picked a duff one yet again.

We kept the windows carefully wound up. Those monkeys had no idea how dangerous Plass children could be.

Our car doesn't like travelling slowly. Mind you, it doesn't much like travelling fast either. In fact, given that its primary function is the provision of transport, it shows a marked reluctance to move at all. Most of all, though, it hates crawling along at a snail's pace. It gets very hot and smokes a great deal and the little temperature thing goes into the red bit and we all get rather jumpy. After we'd left the monkey enclosure we had to stop to let the engine cool down.

Just next to where we stopped, a sparrow was washing itself in a pool of water. The children craned out of the windows to watch and a little line of cars pulled up behind us to see what we were looking at.

The sparrow, sensing a rags-to-riches opportunity, put on the performance of its life; the most sensationally flamboyant piece of sparrow toiletry ever seen.

The other cars drifted slowly round and past us, their occupants looking slightly puzzled. At last we moved on, leaving the sparrow alone with his memories of greatness.

It might never happen again. But he would always know what it meant to be a star. From now on he would hob-nob with lions and swop show-biz anecdotes with warthogs.

Later, we abandoned our gasping vehicle, and set off across a large lake in a motor launch, together with twenty or thirty other people, to see the gorillas.

The two gorillas live on an island in the middle of the lake, and because they tend to become bored and fight they are furnished with their own television set, situated cosily in a little hut.

Their favourite programme, our guide informed us, was *East-Enders*. There was something vaguely hysterical about the idea of a boat load of *East-Enders* watchers peering inquisitively at two *East-Enders*-watching gorillas.

In fact, we could only just see bits of the creatures as they sat beneath a tree, presumably swopping ideas on what life will be like without Dirty Den . . . .

By the time we left the park, we were no clearer in our views on wild creatures in captivity than we had been before, but there was something about the scenes we had witnessed that reminded us irresistibly of something else.

The animals in the safari park get all the food they need, without trying. If they get bored there's always *East-Enders*. It's comfortable, but it's not natural. We saw them, but not at their untamed, resourceful best. The system looks after them and all they have to do is look as if they might do something dramatic.

Lions yawning, monkeys fiddling with cars, gorillas glued to the telly – they could have been Christians in the South-East of England.

I felt guilty. I'd rather be a sparrow . . .

Fear of Mint Sauce

I'm not very good at being tied down when it comes to the subject matter for speaking engagements, especially on those occasions when I am the 'visiting preacher' at a church. I can't preach to save my life – at least, not in any formal sense. I seem to be constitutionally incapable of assembling three points, all beginning with the same letter. You know the sort of thing I mean:

'My sermon this morning is divided into three sections under the headings – Peace, Power and Pork-scratchings. . . .'

You see? I can't even think of a sensible third one just to show you what I mean. I don't know how people do it.

That's why I panicked somewhat when, a year or so ago, I was asked to preach on the text: 'I am the good shepherd.'

As usual, when I've been given a specific title like this, my confidence nose-dived like some spluttering first world war bi-plane. I like big, broad headings that enable me to meander, and explore ideas and tell unrelated stories – those who have heard me speak will know, to their cost, exactly what I mean.

Just before my emotional Sopwith Camel hit the ground (have you ever regretted starting a metaphor?) I discovered a parachute in the form of a small zoo a few miles from our home, known as Drusillas. It isn't a Safari Park like the place I just mentioned, but it's very good. In the course of wandering around with my wife and our own small menagerie (no, I still hadn't worked out what to think about zoos), certain ideas occurred to me. Why, I wondered, did Jesus decide to portray us, his followers, as sheep? After all, the Bible is ankle-deep in all sorts of creatures. In Matthew's gospel Jesus says, 'Behold I send you out as sheep in the midst of wolves; so be wise as serpents and innocent as doves.' Quite a noisy little gathering if they all started bleating and howling and hissing and cooing at the same time.

So, why sheep? Obviously they were much in evidence in that part of the world. Was it just that they were the most available visual aid?

We lingered for a while at the tortoise pen. Twenty or more little armoured tanks were crawling under and over each other to get at the heap of food that had just been left for them. I pictured Jesus standing on a hillside and declaiming, 'I am the good tortoise keeper. My tortoises know my voice, and they come to me – very, very slowly . . . .'

Makes sense, doesn't it, especially when you think of the way Christians retreat into their shells when anything mildly threatening happens? Perhaps there weren't any tortoises in Judea.

The exotic birds who lived by a large, artificial lake suggested other possibilities.

'I am the good flamingo herder. My flamingoes know my voice, but every time anyone stares at them they stand on one leg and turn pink . . . .'

Or the monkey house.

'I am the monkey husbander. My monkeys hear my voice, but they chatter ceaselessly and perform unnecessarily complicated double somersaults whenever it becomes important to move higher or lower . . . .'

The porcupines.

'I am the good porcupine keeper. My porcupines may well know my voice, but they are almost exclusively concerned with defending themselves, and are very difficult to get close to . . . .'

Emus.

'I am the good emu-watcher. My emus know my voice, but they are so used to being grounded, that they've forgotten they were originally designed to fly . . . .'

I could go on for ever; there are lots of different animals and birds at Drusillas, but I'd better get on to the sheep. We came to a small enclosure, strewn with straw, and containing a ewe with her two recently born lambs. These knock-kneed little creatures, looking like something created out of pipe-cleaners, were clearly rather nervous of the spectators who ringed their small temporary home. One was simply standing and quivering beside his mother, while his brother or sister (well, can *you* sex lambs?) had hidden his face behind a small protruding piece of wood. He seemed to believe that if he couldn't see us then we probably couldn't see him. A tinge of ostrich in his ancestry, perhaps? Mother sheep was trembling constantly, her eyes flicking round fearfully from human face to human face. She looked as if she would have loved to find a herd to belong to, and a shepherd, perhaps. Maybe that's why Jesus described us as sheep; because we're nervous things who don't know where to go or who to follow. Milling around in crowds, separated into families, or isolated as individuals, the same shadowy problem has always existed in the hearts of men, women and sheep: 'I know that I belong to someone, but where shall I find that person, and will he greet me with love or mint sauce?'

I have to confess, as a relatively long-term bleater, that for many years I suffered from this mint-sauce view of God. Either he was fattening me for the kill, as it were, or else he was gritting his teeth and allowing me to hang around on the edge of his flock until such time as it became necessary to shoo me off into the wilderness. What a pathetically insecure little sheep I have been.

And now?

Well, I'm suffering a little thinning of the fleece, but the patient guidance of the good shepherd has warmed me into a reassuring confidence that I'm not going to end up on anyone's cosmic dinner table. Nowadays I find the rest of the flock

172

endearing, irritating, puzzling, lovable, confusing and infuriating. I'm sure they have an equally diverse view of me, but the important thing is our awareness that we belong to each other, and that our mutual love and concern are top priorities.

We are a community of hope, not a perfect and triumphant army: unsure about many things, but united by our desires to be good, and a sheep-like dependency upon the good shepherd.

Graffiti
The Devil's Aerosol

It's not easy to shake off the past. Wouldn't it be wonderful if conversion brought immediate, comprehensive repair and transfiguration? Instant perfection.

A bit of a shock for our nearest and dearest, though. Imagine waking up to find that 'Our Fred', whose every vice is as familiar as an old friend, has become a blazing torch of eternal light. Perhaps it wouldn't be so wonderful after all.

But why does the process of change take so long? Why are the labour pains of being born again so prolonged and acute for so many Christian people?

I have a friend whose ministry of healing and counselling has been stunningly effective. He is the smile on the face of God to a procession of needy people, but as his life goes on he is discovering layer upon layer of injury and pain related to the past, particularly in connection with his very early years when he suffered sexual abuse from his mother, and a very unhappy childhood generally.

Many of his buried memories have been uncovered and healed, but there are many more to come. How can we understand this process by which the past puts painful clamps on the present? Let me suggest just one way to look at it. It's summed up by a very modern word – graffiti.

The prophet Jeremiah announced God's intention to write his law on the hearts of his people, and the apostle Paul described the Corinthian Christians as a letter from Christ, written on the tablets of human hearts.

The problem though, assuming your heart is anything like mine, is that the negative graffiti accumulated over the years are so thick and indelible that there's not a great deal of space left for anything else.

The devil wields a pretty effective infernal aerosol can. Let me tell you about some of the scribbles I've discovered.

When I was a little boy of six I decided that I wanted to be an actor when I grew up. I announced this ambition to an aunt who happened to be staying at the time.

'Oh no,' she replied with sparkling auntly wit, 'you need to be good-looking to do that.'

Of course, Auntie Gertrude, or whatever her name was, had no intention of upsetting me – she was just being funny. But it's really and truly no exaggeration to say that the discovery that I was not good-looking wounded my self-image for years.

The next scribble – scraped out in capital letters, this one – happened when I was a teenager. I was in the middle of a combined Drama/GCE course at a college of further education in Tunbridge Wells.

One afternoon, as I sat talking to a couple of other students on the lawn at the back of the building, one of the lecturers strolled over and, quite gratuitously, told me that I was a 'waster'. Whatever chances and opportunities came my way, he said, I would misuse and simply waste. Then he strolled off.

I think he was trying to be helpful, but, as we all know, the road to Hell is paved with good intentions – or unposted letters in my wife's case – and those few words of his came very close to snuffing out the tiny spark of confidence that glowed faintly in my very insecure teenage heart.

Over the years that sentence has haunted me, and it has never had a constructive effect. It has often weakened my resolve, and still does very occasionally.

Sometimes the graffiti are in the form of conversational ruts, the same sort of verbal dialogue repeated again and again, eroding self-confidence and casting a shadow of defeat over the future.

Consider the following scene, for example, between a daughter and her father.

Daughter: Did you manage to get my bike done, Dad?

Father: I'm changing this plug for your mother, I've just mended the chair that your brother broke, and I've had your Auntie Phyllis on the phone for twenty minutes about next Wednesday. No, I have not got round to your bike yet and it's no use going on about it because I just haven't had time!

Daughter: I didn't mean you should have done it, Dad. I was just asking —

Father: Everyone's just asking. I've told you I'll do it, and I will do it just as soon as I can, so you'll just have to be patient.

Daughter: I don't mind being patient, Dad. I wasn't complaining about you not doing it, I was just wondering if you had got round to it. It was just . . . information I wanted.

Father: Okay! All right! I'll leave the plug. Let's not bother about what anybody else wants. Let's just get your bike fixed then you'll be all right and we can start seeing to other people's needs.

Daughter: But I don't want you to do my bike now. I told you, I was just . . .'.

Father: Well, if you don't want me to do your bike now, why have you been getting so het-up about it?

Daughter: I haven't been getting het-up about it! I wasn't anything when I first came in!

Father: *Well, what are you shouting at me for if you're not het-up?*

Daughter: I *wasn't* het-up!

Father: Well, you certainly are now, aren't you? Or is this what you call being calm and peaceful?

Daughter: Dad, when I came in I simply asked you quite quietly and nicely whether you'd done my bike or not. That's all I wanted to know — had you done my bike.

Father: Well, have you moved all your books off the landing yet?

Daughter: No, but that's not what we're talking about!

Father: Oh, I see! We're allowed to talk about me not having done what you wanted, but we're not allowed to talk about you letting me down. Don't you think that's a bit less than fair?

(PAUSE)

Daughter: That's stupid, Dad!

Father: Ah! Now we come it it, don't we? We usually end up with me being stupid don't we? Do you know what my father would have said to me if I'd ever *dared* to talk to him like that?

Daughter: I –

Father: Well, do you?

Daughter: (DEAD TONES) Yes, I do. You've told me about thirty-nine times. He'd have taken all your privileges away for the next two weeks, and you might have got the strap as well.

Father: There's no need to be sarcastic about your grandfather. At least he never set out to cause trouble in the family. He was a good man who never did less than his best. He loved you kids when you were little, and I'd be ashamed to have him standing here listening to the way you're going on! I don't know why you do it!

I don't know what's happened to you! We used to play games and have a laugh together. You used to look up to me and ask questions and I'd show you how to do things – we were best friends, dammit! What have I done to deserve you drifting off into being Miss Clever-clever?

Daughter: Dad – please! It's not fair. I didn't start any of this!

Father: Oh, you didn't start it. Who did then? The man in the moon? You come in here demanding that I do your blessed bike, you tell me I'm stupid when I talk about other people's needs, you mock your grandfather who's dead and can't defend himself, and then you tell me you didn't start any of it! Well, I'm sorry but I think I'm too stupid to understand that, much too stupid!

Daughter: (ALMOST BREATHLESS WITH HURT) Look, Dad, I came in, right? And I said – exactly like this – I said, 'Have you managed to do my bike, Dad?' and you got all exasperated and went on about all the other things you had to do, but I – wasn't – complaining. I – was – just – asking . . . .

Father: Yes, like I've *just* been asking you for weeks and weeks to clear your books and stuff off the landing, and help your mother round the house and think about others a bit more than you do –

Daughter: (FURIOUS) That's not what we were talking about! That's not what we were talking about! You stupid, stupid man! You don't want to understand! You don't want to listen to what I'm saying! I didn't start it! I didn't start it! I didn't start it! (SHE CONTINUES TO SHOUT THOSE THREE WORDS OVER AND OVER AGAIN)

Father: (CALLS HIS WIFE) Sheila! Come and lend a hand. Dorothy's having one of her does again!

Mother: Come on, Dotty, calm down, you'll only make your throat sore, calm down love, there's no point.

Father: She's hysterical!
(HE SMACKS HER ONCE ON THE FACE. SHE IMMEDIATELY STOPS SHOUTING).

I could make a long list of the graffiti that clutter my heart space. So could you. Things people have said, failures that have destroyed confidence, traumatic experiences, profound, unforgettable embarrassments – all sorts of things. Usually each one tells you a lie about yourself:

- You will never succeed.
- You are not lovable.
- God has cast you aside because of *that* sin.
- You're boring.
- People will only ever use you.
- Happiness is impossible.
- Your life has no purpose.

The almost invariable untruthfulness of these scrawlings should be sufficient indication of their ultimate authorship.

The father of lies is anxious that our souls should be covered by a confused mass of misinformation, some of it so deeply scored that it comes close to breaking our hearts.

Jesus promises that we shall be washed as white as snow. This may involve several years' work by the divine cleaning department in the case of you and me, but we have the promise and therefore we have the hope as well.

We may, like the friend I mentioned earlier, need specific healing of memories, we may just need to be loved for a good long time.

One of the things I like about God, and I've only discovered it relatively recently, is that he has relationships, not systems. When someone is converted he doesn't say, 'Right, Fred's come to faith, procedure number 39B, line 6, get on it, angels!'

He says, 'Fred's come home to me – wonderful! Now let's have a think about this. Old Fred's an awkward customer in some ways. Too much pressure and he just slips out sideways. What we need to do is . . . .'

And so a plan, specially, particularly designed for Fred, is set in motion. It will offer the best possible options, guidance and influence, and it will be alive with the love of God. Fred may mess it up at various points, but the plan is flexible and can be adjusted by Fred's new parent.

If God was a tailor there would be no off-the-peg suits in his shop, only bespoke ones, meticulously cut and designed to provide a perfect fit for each individual customer.

Our heavenly father knows everything there is to know about us, every worry, every hurt, every tiny scar, every line of graffiti that is trespassing in our lives. Let's try to relax a little, and ask him to show us his plan for clearing a space in our hearts.

The Worst Crime in the World
'What do you think is the worst crime in the world?'

One of my children asked me that question once, probably during Sunday lunch – they save up all their most difficult questions for Sunday lunchtime. I don't think I produced a very satisfactory answer at the time, but there probably is no final answer to a question like that, not one that everyone would agree with anyway. It made me think, though.

What is the worst crime in the world?

One of G. K. Chesterton's Father Brown stories is actually entitled *The Worst Crime in the World*. In this tale the ultimate sin was patricide, the murder of a father by his son, revealed as usual through the penetrating insights of the modest little Roman Catholic priest called Brown.

I imagine that many people would agree with this answer to my original question, the suggestion that illegal killing is the very worst thing that one could do, especially the kind of murder that Chesterton is describing.

The fact is, however, that a person's perception of what constitutes truly evil behaviour is very often conditioned by his or her particular circumstances and experiences.

I remember reading a book on the philosophy of education as part of my teacher-training course. I only understood one sentence in fifty, but it included a little anecdote that has stayed in my mind ever since. A class of junior children were given the task, by their teacher, of listing the ten worst things that anyone could do, in descending order of 'badness'.

Notable among the results of this exercise, was the list of a child who had written:

1. Murder.
2. Shouting in the corridor.

The latter sin never quite made it into the ten commandments, but for that child, it clearly ranked high above theft, adultery, and all the other trivial misdemeanours that our weak flesh is capable of. I'm rather glad I didn't go to that school.

Or, consider the case of a teenage boy whom we used to know. Alan was a frequent visitor to the little semi-detached house in Bromley that my wife and I shared with the curate of St Augustine's church, an old friend of mine called John Hall. None of us had any money, so the house was furnished, in the main, with items that had already been sold three or four times at the annual scout jumble sale. Indeed, local people who came to the house would often point out, with nostalgic pleasure, some item of furniture that had once been theirs.

Alan's house, by contrast, was like something out of a glossy magazine. His mother was not just house-proud, she was fanatically devoted to the brushing and dusting and scrubbing and hoovering of the brick-built god whom she served. Her family were annoying infidels who constantly undid all her good works.

Each evening, after the family meal, this sad woman insisted that her husband and son sat on camp chairs (fetched from an immaculate cupboard under the stairs) in order to avoid using the three-piece suite, her special pride and joy. Occasionally, she would arrive home to discover a tiny wrinkle in the fabric of the settee or armchair, and would then, in scandalised and accusatory tones, utter the immortal words: 'Someone's been sitting on the chairs!'

Unsurprisingly, Alan was a rather tense lad, though very pleasant company. He visited us a lot, perhaps because we were less than house-proud, to put it mildly, and not very bothered about 'things'. One day, however, he clearly thought that he had committed the worst crime in the world in the middle of our sitting-room.

Not long after our first meeting, he came in for coffee one morning, and, perfectly reasonably, sat down on an upright wooden chair beside the table. This chair was part of our latest jumble sale acquisition, a set of four heavily worn dining-room chairs which had cost the huge sum of five pence each. They had undoubtedly arrived at their final resting place.

As Alan relaxed his weight onto the chair he had selected, it collapsed completely, immediately and irreparably. It was no longer a chair and would never be a chair again.

Alan gazed up at us from the midst of the wreckage, physically unhurt as far as we could see, but white-faced with horror as he waited to see what our response would be to this abominable crime. After all, in his house, world war three broke out if you *sat* in the wrong chair. What kind of armageddon would erupt now that he had totally demolished one?

The expression on Alan's face as Bridget and I fell about laughing, moved from shock, through bewilderment to profound relief. We weren't about to beat him to death with a piece of ex-furniture. He really relaxed in our house after that.

I'm afraid that many Christians have a problem similar to that of Alan, and the child in the junior class. They have never committed the huge, cataclysmic sins or crimes such as murder, but they do have their own specific sin, vice or problem, which can easily seem like the worst crime in the world, depending on who supplied your moral yardstick in the first place. The junior child's was supplied by his teacher, Alan's by his mother, but it could be a denominational emphasis, or the influence of one Christian leader or parent or adviser.

It was a great relief to me, when I encountered one of these personal blocks, to go back to the gospels and remind myself of what I already knew in my heart.

Jesus condemned *all* sin. If the disciples were hoping for a bit of relaxation on some points then they must have been very disappointed indeed. You can't even lust after a woman in your heart, he told his followers. You are damned if you call your brother a fool, he went on to say. Far from easing up on the rules, he made Moses look like an anarchist. Not only did he not abolish the law, he made it absolutely clear that the standard demanded by God is *so* high that no one (except himself) had any chance of achieving that standard, let alone maintaining it.

Then, having made it clear that no human being would ever qualify for entry into the Kingdom of God, he voluntarily went to his death to save us from the consequences of breaking that law which he had insisted we must obey to the letter; very eccentric behaviour indeed for anyone but the Son of God.

As though it were a vast lake, we see only the surface of this mysterious act of atonement, but there is no doubt that if the sins of murder and messing up an armchair are thrown simultaneously into that serene expanse of water, they will sink at the same speed, and they will disappear with the same merciful certainty that they are gone for ever.

Failing to take advantage of that opportunity is probably the worst crime in the world – against ourselves.

Picking up the Pieces

Those who know Winchester Cathedral well, will be aware that it contains a quite extraordinary jigsaw puzzle.

Now, I'm something of an expert when it comes to jigsaws. I've got four children (which is about ten more than three, for those who don't know), and they range from cool sixteen to totally dominant three-and-a-half.

Sixteen years of assorted jigsaw puzzles have passed through the hands, toy-shelves and cracks in the floorboards of our offspring. Some are the very simple, thick kind that come in four pieces – those are the ones that little Katy or I do – and others are the huge two-thousand-piece sort where the sky drives you raving mad and the last three pieces look as if they couldn't *possibly* fit, but they do.

In a china pot upstairs I've got a sad little collection of orphaned jigsaw pieces. I can't help it! I can't bring myself to throw them away. I find them under stair-carpets, or blocking up the hoover, or even in the garden. They have a certain desolate, dog-eared charm, and, besides, any one of them might, one day, enable me to heal the anguish of some member of the family who has finished a long and difficult jigsaw only to find that ONE PIECE IS MISSING! Those lost pieces have a place somewhere and I just have this pathetic hope that they'll get back where they belong eventually, and mean something again.

Winchester Cathedral's spectacular jigsaw puzzle is, in fact, a huge window in the west wall, but it's unlike any other church window that I've ever seen. It appears to be made up of hundreds of pieces of glass, each of which is a different shape and size, but there is no overall picture or pattern. If you look very carefully you will see a foot, or part of a face, or some other small detail, but the sections of glass are arranged in such a random fashion that they seem to make no sense at all. Those who know the history of the cathedral will tell you that, once upon a time, they did make sense, and then something happened.

It was the seventeenth century and Cromwell's forces were in the process of securing the country for their leader. When the Puritan army came to Winchester many of the most beautiful works of art in the cathedral were brutally destroyed. The west window was completely smashed.

Aghast at this appalling act of vandalism, some of the local people collected the pieces of glass and hid them carefully, intending to put the window back when the soldiers had gone or the religious climate had relaxed a little.

When that time came, though, the task proved too difficult. Willing as the townsfolk were, they simply couldn't do it. That enormous jigsaw puzzle was too much for them. But that must have been a very stubborn group of people indeed. Their window was going back into the west wall of Winchester Cathedral whether it made sense or not! So, back it went, with the fragments of glass fastened together in crazy disarray, and there it still is, a monument to determination and community spirit.

Some people (Christian or otherwise) seem to float through life with few storms or disturbances to disrupt their progress. Whatever the reasons for this – temperament, background, personality or particular circumstances, I rejoice for these fortunate ones, but I also grieve for those who seem to encounter continual suffering.

For many people who read these words life may seem to have disintegrated, just as that vast window did more than three hundred years ago, into a jigsaw puzzle that doesn't seem to make any sense at all. I've been through that process of falling apart myself, and I know about the sobbing despair that can fill the nights and days with what feels like endless darkness. There are two things that might be worth considering.

First, like me at home, I feel quietly sure that God picks up and keeps the sad, lost parts of his suffering children's lives because he knows that they are pieces of the completed puzzle, however much of a mystery they may seem at the moment.

Secondly, it may be helpful to think about that cathedral window once again. Somewhere in that strange jumble of shattered images a potential picture still exists. We may not see it in its former state, not this side of heaven at any rate, but we know for sure that it is there. It is, I believe, not too optimistic to trust that the same God who says, 'Behold, I make all things new' will take every fragment – good and bad – of our disintegrated lives, and show us one day what an unexpectedly beautiful picture they were always intended to make.

Mary, the mother of Jesus, has always been a personal heroine of mine in this respect. Her personal collection of, apparently, unmatched jigsaw pieces was strange indeed.

First of all, as a young, unmarried girl, she is visited by an angel who announces that she is to become pregnant by the Holy Ghost. What an irregular shape to begin with! It was just as well that Joseph had it all authenticated by his own angelic visitor.

The next bit of the puzzle comes when Mary arrives in Bethlehem only to find that she is forced to bed down in a smelly old stable. She might easily have said, 'Look, God, this is a bit off! Are you losing your grip? You've blown the budget on the angels, there's nothing left for bed and breakfast.' But she didn't say that. Unlike many of us modern Christians she accepted everything that came alone – puzzled but willing.

After the birth of Jesus the other pieces of the puzzle came thick and fast; shepherds turning up to see the baby – very nice, but why? Wise men arriving with strange symbolic gifts; the meeting with Simeon in the temple; the flight into Egypt to escape Herod; the death of all those babies in Bethlehem.

Much later comes the business of the boy Jesus absenting himself from his parents' care for three days, to be discovered eventually discussing religious matters with doctors of the law.

'Didn't it occur to you', says Jesus to his distraught mother, 'that I would be in my father's house?'

The Bible says that Mary stored all these things in her heart, rather like the contents of that little pot of mine, lots of oddly shaped bits of jigsaw that seemed to mean very little at the time. Sometimes, when things are quiet, she must have taken those pieces out – as it were – and tried to fit them together. Some of them so starkly contrasted:

'Blessed art thou among women . . . .'

'A sword shall pierce thy heart also . . . .'

Then, when Jesus begins his ministry, there are the miracles and the conflicts, the teaching and the taking on of a very powerful establishment; the pain of hearing him say, 'Who is my mother?'; and that magical moment when, almost with his last breath, he looks at her from the cross with loving eyes and instructs one of his disciples to look after her when he is gone.

As she mourned at the foot of that cross, Mary must have wondered if the jigsaw would ever be completed now.

We seldom talk about it in the Church, but can you imagine Mary's feelings when she first saw her son alive and well three days after his dead body had been placed in the tomb? That moment, and the moment when the Holy Spirit came in tongues of flame and a mighty rushing wind, must have seemed like the last two pieces of the picture, a picture that showed Mary she had played a leading part in bringing God himself into the world, so that generation after generation would be able to go home to their heavenly father.

But, of course, the final piece of the jigsaw, for Mary and for each of us, must be our encounter with Jesus in the place where he sits at the right hand of his father. When that happens the picture will certainly be complete, but it may be very different from what we expected.

If you ever find yourself in Winchester, visit the cathedral for half an hour – take a look at that window . . .

Heaven
Far Pavilions?

For me, April shines like a jewel in the fascinating necklace of the year. It makes me think of two very important things. First, it's the time of year when God switches on the heavenly sprinkler system to prepare our cricket pitches for a new season.

I might possibly have let slip in previous writings a hint of the passion I feel for this superlative activity. If we were not Christians my three sons and I would undoubtedly worship the sport god, an energetic trinity composed of cricket, football and rugby.

For me, the greatest of these is cricket, so the alternative shine and shower of the fourth month fills me annually with exuberant expectancy and sends me burrowing through the junk in the cupboard under the stairs muttering things like, 'I know I put that bat in here! I just wish people wouldn't move things . . . .'

It's always where I left it, and I always find it, and I always stand for a moment caressing the wood with the tips of my fingers, making little half-witted cooing sounds as my mind is filled with anticipation of the red, white, green and blue of a perfect cricketing day.

'Earth hath not anything to show more fair . . . .' Oh, no, that's the view from Westminster Bridge isn't it? Sorry!

Now, in case you think this is all a bit over the top, I do realise that, for some people, cricket is the most excruciatingly effective cure for insomnia ever devised by man. But then, I might find your favourite activity completely incomprehensible.

Perhaps you are devoted to wrestling with aardvarks. I respect that. My ignorance of the finer points of aardvark wrestling may prohibit me from enjoying it as you do, but I understand enjoyment. Let us be tolerant of each other.

The second thing that April makes me think of is heaven.

I live almost at the base of the South Downs, which means that I'm constantly being drawn to the top of the South Downs. God goes up there a lot too, and I walk and talk with him if we meet.

We've also met in police cells and pubs and dark, dangerous places, but this is a different kind of encounter. Up on those swelling green hills in springtime I can taste the bubbling springs of heaven as I sense his yearning for the return of perfection to the world he made so long ago. I need those encounters because I've had trouble with the idea of heaven.

Perhaps I'm the only one who has experienced these fears about the after-life, but I doubt it.

Sometimes, on a Sunday morning, whatever the denominational setting, I have known a sudden surging panic as I imagine heaven being like an average morning service, but going on for ever. A small child inside me shouts, 'I don't want to go! I don't want to go!'

Then there are some of the rewards promised by scripture, many of them items in a sort of regulation Paradise kit, things like gold crowns and white robes. No doubt these were powerful incentives to Jesus' contemporaries, mainly poor folk enduring the humiliating fact of Roman occupation, but they don't attract me at all. I'd just as soon walk the golden streets of heaven in jeans, tee-shirt and no head covering at all if the divine quartermaster doesn't mind.

I find it interesting to conjecture how Jesus might have described heaven if he had entered the world as a man at the present stage in history. I feel sure that he would have selected symbols relevant to the age, but I wonder if he might have focused in on my particular preoccupation. Sometimes, in the course of those hill-top walks of mine, I have addressed God on the subject of life after death and the specific components of eternal bliss.

'God,' I've said, 'I don't really want a gold crown like it says in the Bible. I don't fancy sitting round for eternity singing choruses and – and all the other things.

'I like – love – so many things on this earth you made. When the new earth gets done, couldn't I have a little flat a bus-ride from The Oval? I love you, and I want to be with you, but . . . .'

Up on the hills I can hear God chuckling when I say that. 'The essence of everything you have loved will be yours', he says. 'Trust me. No eye has seen, no ear has heard, no mind has conceived what God has prepared for those who love him.'

And when I think about those words calmly and sensibly the truth is so obvious. Why should I expect God, who knows me and loves me like the best possible of fathers, to saddle me for ever with a burden of tedium and monotony? How intriguing to reflect that heaven is certain to contain the essence of all those things that I have loved and cared about most. What a joy it must be for our Heavenly Father to arrange individual mansions for each of his beloved children as they come to him, welcome visitors in his kingdom because the name of Jesus is always on their lips.

Suddenly it all begins to seem rather exciting.

Cricket and heaven – perhaps they're not mutually exclusive after all. We shall see . . .'.

I'm dying to live after living has ended,
I'm living for life after death,
Alive to the fact that I'm dead apprehensive,
I'll live to the end of my breath.
But what would life be were I no longer living,
And death were no longer alive,
How would I stick it without my cricket,
How would I ever survive?
Would I cross swords on some heavenly Lords,
With the angels of Holding and Hall,

Would I face up to Lillee without feeling silly,
And even catch sight of the ball?
Would a man with a beard who the bowlers all
    feared,
Redeem us from losing – a sin?
Yes, by Grace we'd be saved as his century
    paved
The way to a glorious win.
I promise you Lord, I'll never get bored,
I'll practise the harp, there, I've sworn,
If cricket's allowed, I'll be back on my cloud,
The moment that stumps have been drawn.

How easy it is for our image of heaven to be
distorted and darkened by the kinds of pictures
and stories that insist on hanging sterile religious
trappings over attractive Christian realities. Don't
get down about the after-life; it'll be heaven!

We'll Meet Again

Part of the joy of heaven will be reunion with
people we loved in this life.

My friend, Chris, loved his mother very much.
Widowed relatively early in life, she eventually
became unwell, and was diagnosed as having an
incurable disease. Chris and his wife Jean nursed
her through the final stages of what turned out to
be a rapidly spreading, wasting disease, until she
died in the spare bedroom of their little house in
Eastbourne.

It was a complex experience for Chris. The
pain of watching his mother's suffering was almost unbearable, especially as she grew thinner

and thinner, and more and more helpless. Increasingly, he felt as if he was parent in the relationship, and his mother a child, a child whose physical dependency became more pronounced with every week that passed. Occasionally his emotions would overwhelm him and he would sob uncontrollably at the side of the bed, forced into being a child again by the power of his grief. At such times, his mother was able to reach out an enfeebled hand and comfort him with her touch. Her mind and emotions were perfectly sound, and she knew exactly what her son was going through. Through this continual exchange of caring and receiving roles the relationship deepened and sweetened in a way that was quite new to both of them.

Death, when it came, did not seem harsh, and it certainly didn't feel like the end. United on one very important level by their Christian faith, Chris and his mother said their farewells in the sure and certain knowledge that they would meet again, not as parent and child perhaps, but in a new and more complete relationship. Some time after his mother's death, Chris asked me if I might write something about his feelings and experiences during those last few difficult weeks. The following poem is an inadequate attempt to do just that.

I mothered she who mothered me,
The body that I never knew,
(Though she knew mine so well when I was
small and she was all my need).

So plaintive now,
Her arms surrendered high to be undressed or
   dressed,
Like some poor sickly child,
Who sees no shame in helplessness,
Embarrassed once, but all too happy now,
To let me ease her weariness.
And yet, when I collapsed and cried beside her
   on the bed,
She was my mother once again,
She reached her hand out to the child in me,
She dried my tears,
And held me there till I was still.
So ill, so long
Until, at last, when endless days of hopefulness
   had faded finally
There came a night of harmony, a night of
   many psalms,
I mothered she who mothered me
And laid my sister gently
In our father's arms.

Love or Light-Sabres

I am told by some people that the anticipation of
union with Jesus will overcome fear of death. The
answers, they say, are in the scriptures. I don't
believe it is quite as simple as that.

When I was converted nearly twenty-five years
ago I began, with many others, a lifelong attempt
to understand what the Bible means, or should
mean, to Christians like myself.

Like many young Christians in the sixties I
began by swallowing whole lumps of information

without really chewing or digesting the things that I was told. Thus, at the tender age of sixteen, I was loudly and dogmatically arguing that the Bible was without question inerrant and infallible, and that anyone who disagreed with me was probably not saved and certainly in grave error.

As the years pass though, and I gradually learn how to relax into a genuine father-son relationship with God, I've come to realise that it can take decades for knowledge to become truly heartfelt. In my own journey towards understanding I have reached the point where I know in my heart that the Bible is a letter from God to me, and every word is meant to be there. It begins: 'Dear Adrian . . .', and it ends: 'Love, God'. I thank him for it.

Back in those early days also, I had what seems on reflection to have been a somewhat superstitious belief in the 'magical' power of scripture verses, again a distorted perception of a truth that was taught in an over-simplified manner. I developed, or inherited, or caught, the notion that in any problematic situation it was possible to wield portions of the Bible rather like the light sabres used in *Star Wars*.

On the many occasions when my holy incantations didn't work, I assumed that either I had backslidden in some way, or that I had picked the wrong scripture, or, after particularly dismal failures, that there was no God after all. I still understand virtually nothing, but my understanding in this area has at least matured a little.

It seems to me now that there are indeed times when scripture can be used like a sword to cut through worldly or satanic thickets, but it is not automatic and if we are, like Jesus, doing only what we see the father doing, it can never be a loose or random way of approaching problems. Sometimes we are given a specific scripture, not to thrust dramatically under someone's nose, but to show us what we must do. Let me give you an example of what I mean.

At the end of last year a man called Peter, whom I know a little, dropped round for coffee. Peter is a retired U.R.C. minister, a good man and a solid Christian. As we sipped our coffee he told me that his wife, Jean, had died two days previously. She had been ill for some time, finally discharging herself from hospital three years ago, a few months before Peter was due to retire. She had come home to die.

The illness was incurable and she was very frightened. As Peter lay beside his wife in the darkness, on the first night of her return, he asked himself and God what he could possibly do to ease the suffering of this woman who had given in to the prospect of imminent death, and whose body was rigid with the terror of its approach.

People talk very easily about receiving 'words from the Lord'. When little hangs on the outcome it can be a very inexpensive claim to make. That night, for one of the very few times in his life, Peter believed that God had placed a verse of scripture into his mind, and that it was connected somehow with his desperate prayer.

What was the verse? It was a very familiar one; one he had read and even spoken about many times in the course of his long preaching career. It occurs in the first epistle of John, and consists of just five words: 'Perfect love casts out fear.'

But what did it mean? Some people, well-meaning no doubt, would have switched the light on, and cheerily cried: 'Good news! The Lord's given me a word for you – "Perfect love casts out fear". Feeling better?'

But Peter didn't see it like that. The word had been for him, not Jean. He was supposed to do something. By the morning he knew what it was, and he knew how costly it would be; tremendous emotional expenditure on someone he was bound to lose eventually.

Peter cuddled Jean for breakfast and he cuddled her for lunch, he cuddled her for tea and he cuddled her for supper. For three months he was rarely more than three yards away from her. Maybe it wasn't perfect love, but it was the very best he'd got, and God was in it. At the end of that three months the fear had been loved out of Jean, and she was beginning to take an interest in where she and Peter might live after his retirement.

Peter held his wife's hand three years later as she died in late December, and knew as he did so that the fear was gone from her. He was able to say to God: 'I did do it, Lord. I did what you said. It might not have been perfect love, but I did my best and you topped it up. You were right in what you told me that night. Thank you. . . .'

Peter's experience highlights a truth that I have paid lip-service to for years without really absorbing its importance. Namely, that God will do what he will do, for his own good reasons, and that these 'doings' will frequently fail to fit with the personal theology I have cobbled together over the years. Peter and his wife needed that particular word, applied in that particular way, at that particular time, and God knew it.

Similarly, a friend of mine who is a pentecostal minister (his only fault!), was anxious that his father should become a Christian. With customary energy he set about expounding the scriptures to his ageing parent, threatening him with hell, promising him heaven, and generally giving him the 'works'. After a lengthy experience of this kind of approach the old man did his best to be out when he knew his son was likely to call. Conversion was definitely not on *his* agenda.

It was only when my friend stopped talking and started listening that God was able to whisper to him: 'When did you last tell your dad you loved him?'

'Never', thought my friend. 'I should have done, but I never have . . .'

The next day he went along to see his father, put his arm round his shoulders and, ignoring the flinch of resistance to what his dad obviously thought was going to be yet another evangelical blast, said those three words that are so difficult to use when they are not common conversational currency: 'I love you.'

My friend's father made a Christian commitment very shortly after that, and became a member of his own son's church.

God knows what will melt hearts much better than we do, and it may be different in every case. I hate the thought that my pet formulae might obscure or postpone the work that the Holy Spirit wants to do. Perhaps, rather, we should aim (as my friend Jo Marriott puts it) to find out what God is doing, and then join in.

He wants people in heaven much more than we do, and he knows how to achieve it.

Outsiders
What Oscar Did

'I never read anything but the Bible. That's the only book I need.'

I have heard that comment more than once whilst visiting churches or groups as a speaker. One shiny-eyed character informed me of this fact as I sat behind a table piled high with my own volumes, signing books for a steady stream of folk who had just endured more than an hour of my voice.

I tried to look abashed. At first this kind of restricted literary diet seemed as though it must be right. Then I was suddenly annoyed with myself. Of course it wasn't right! The depth and richness and beauty of good literature is a gift from God to be used and enjoyed. Obviously, some types of writing (the badly written as much as the obscene) are unhelpful, to say the least, but the secrets of the human heart are unveiled through the literary art in ways that are as diverse as they are enlightening.

By all means let us be selective, but let us not be narrow or prudish.

I wonder, for example, how my friend who only reads the Bible would view my choice of Richard Ellmann's biography of Oscar Wilde, as my favourite book of the last two or three years. It warmed my heart, and I would like to explain *why* it meant so much to me.

Some things never change.

As a small child I occasionally chanced upon a book so ravishingly, richly absorbing, that all I wanted was to inhabit that small universe within a universe, to the exclusion of all other activities and interests. My first choice reading spot was the foot of a pine tree at the top of a hill a mile from my home. That place is all houses now, but I still retreat a mile back from the front of my mind when the book is right and the phone is dead and the family are out and I haven't passed my latest deadline. I hardly left my pine tree from the moment I began to read Richard Ellmann's generous biography.

'What Oscar Wilde Did' was one in a long catalogue of pieces of information withheld by my parents and other adults until I was old

enough to understand. The politics of embarrassment, of course, but I didn't know that. I
adored the beautiful fairy stores, the sparkling
wit of the plays, and the shivering mystery of
poems like *The Harlot's House*, which I loved for its
sounds. My other heroes, Dylan Thomas and
G.K. Chesterton, must have been equally problematic for my parents and early teachers. A

homosexual, an alcoholic and a Jew-hater (what a load of rubbish by the way). They produced humour, beauty and excitement; all the things that proceed from and please the heart of God, and that was all I cared about really.

Crudely nudging my wife into buying Ellmann's book was the first step in my long-saved-up intention to find out about the man, as opposed to the works, which have been affirmed by time in a way that few other literary products of the period can equal. My fascination survived my ignorance (it is a very scholarly and erudite work) because the biographer is warm, witty and compassionate, not just about his subject, who turns out to be an unexpectedly kind and lovable personality in any case, but about the whole array of singular characters and events that gave flavour to the end of the Victorian age.

Oscar Wilde was made for television. There seems little doubt that his legendary skill as wit and raconteur is hardly exaggerated. At its best, there seems to have been an awesome power and fluency in his conversation, which left listeners breathless with excitement and admiration.

'An Audience with Oscar Wilde' would certainly have placed Dame Edna and even the excellent Peter Ustinov firmly in the shade. The 'box' would also have kept Oscar from penury. At most key points in his life he lacked funds and owed money. A generous man, he spent freely and saved nothing. His major talent was not so much in doing as in being. At the end of the last century there was no highly lucrative means of cashing in on verbal and stylistic pyrotechnics, even if you hadn't been exposed by that hypocritical nineties society as the only homosexual in the universe. Wilde would have endeared himself to modern mass audiences, not just because he was a brilliant mind, but because he was not harsh and he was always able and willing to attack his own arguments. Ellmann describes how, on an occasion when some fortune hunter launched a long and vicious verbal attack on the great man, Wilde sat 'like a lump', too kind to triumph in debate by using cruelty.

His downfall lay in his relationships, and a strange, tragic inability to withdraw from situations that were bound to hurt him. In particular, of course, it was his relationship with Lord Alfred Douglas that resulted in so much pain, of which the prison sentence was only a part. Wilde was unable to resist the greedy, beautiful, raging, cruel Douglas, who, in retrospect, seems such a slight object for such a self-damaging obsession. It is not a new story, and it is not about homosexuality. It is about being human and vulnerable.

Ellmann's detailed description of the last few exiled weeks in Paris made me weep. In particular I was moved by an account by Frédéric Boutet, a writer, of encountering Wilde seated at a café in torrential rain, soaked to the skin but unable to move because he had no money to pay for the three or four drinks that had postponed his return to squalid lodgings.

'Like dear St Francis of Assisi I am wedded to poverty,' said Oscar, 'but in my case the marriage is not a success . . . .'

Wilde died on 30th November 1900, his ever faithful friend Robert Ross at his side. He raised his hand shortly before his death when asked if he wished to be received into the Roman Catholic Church, and was baptised, annointed and absolved by the priest who had been called by a worried Robbie.

What does a Jesus-loving relativist like me make of such a life? Wilde told Percival Almy that Christ was not divine. 'It would', he said, 'place too broad a gulf between him and the human soul.' Most people's religion was too vulnerable to the quickness of his perception. Organised expressions of spiritual belief appealed to him as art and something more – he kneeled honestly to at least two priests and the pope – but as Ellmann points out, his views were scarcely orthodox.

The biographer in this case clearly loves his subject, and I believe that he succeeded in making me love him too. Love is *despite* as well as *because of*. Some aspects of Wilde's life repel me, but to understand all is to forgive all. God knows the details of Oscar Wilde's life better than I do, better even than Richard Ellmann. A hand raised just before death may be as efficacious as a few words from a thief dying on a cross. I hope so.

I would like to meet Oscar Wilde in heaven, and, as our God is gracious, I probably will.

Artistic Licence

Any attempt to form Christians into groups that have a secular focus is fraught with problems and dangers.

Not least among these is the tendency for such groups to become congregations after only a few meetings. Because there is no pressure to do specifically religious things, group members can sometimes feel an unexpected freedom to talk about the things that are puzzling or troubling them in their personal lives.

This is fine if the group is equipped and willing to deal with each other's 'entrail-displays', but it can be very frustrating to go along one evening, anxious to learn about the inner workings of the combustion engine, and to end up instead learning about the inner workings of Mabel Drummond.

Perhaps there is a lesson for the Church here. Church leaders who decide to re-title Evening Prayer 'Bee-keeping for Beginners' will probably find the church packed with people who want to talk and sing about God, and who couldn't care less about bees. People are confusing creatures.

A further danger is, or can be, the presence of a self-appointed spiritual chaperone, someone who feels 'burdened' to ensure that communal flirtations with, for instance, something as flighty as art, are not allowed to develop into vulgar and inappropriate relationships.

There is no defence for this kind of re-routing of other people's interests when they have met specifically to pursue those interests, even when the works of art in question are non-religious or, indeed, anti-religious. A communist may tour a stately home without being stripped of his red tie. In fact, he may emerge from his excursion into the world of the privileged classes even more determined than before to carry out his crusade for equality.

Apart from anything else, we need breadth of vision and involvement in the Church. Jesus himself was as fully integrated with the real world as he was untainted by it. There are few things less attractive than what Bernard Levin once called 'single-issue fanaticism', especially as practised by those Christians who tread the bleak, antiseptic passages of religiosity.

I belong to a Christian arts group myself, a regional branch of the Arts Centre Group, a London-based organisation that caters for Christians in the professional and semi-professional arts. Our local group has managed to survive and overcome most of the difficulties that such gatherings are prone to, including, from time to time, the ones that I've just mentioned. In the five years or so that we have been in existence, though, we have seen a bewildering variety of situations and personalities.

Any similarity between those personalities and the ones mentioned in the following verses is, naturally, entirely coincidental.

Our local Christian Arts Group
Meets at St Virginia's Hall,

The cost is not prohibitive,
You pay a pound, that's all.
It started last September
And it's been tremendous fun,
We meet alternate Fridays,
And we share what we have done.
Comments must be true or kind
For nobody is barred,
They range from 'Yes, that's really good!'
To 'Gosh, you have worked hard!'

There's Mrs Leith from Brassey Heath,
Divorced but never low,
Whose bosom mountainously shrouds
The fires down below.
Her many giant canvases
Are mostly purple sky,
She paints in tinted marmite,
No, we haven't asked her why.
At home her neon works of art
Are hanging high and low,
We've often wondered why her husband
Took so long to go.

Miss Duncalk from Cheyne Walk
Is very thin and tense,
She is a Carl André fan
She thinks his bricks make sense.
She educates our appetites
With extracts from Camus,
She says we get a lot from it –
We all pretend we do.
In matters of philosophy

She briskly puts us right,
We hope her inner comprehension
Keeps her warm at night.

Mr Grange is slightly strange
He's something small in eggs,
He always says 'The yolk's on me'
And looks at ladies' legs.
He brings along his only sketch
It's called *Reclining Nude*,
He says it is aesthetic,
But it's not, it's very rude.
Mrs Blair, our acting Chair,
Says, 'Yes, he's less than sound,
But unlike some more pure in heart,
He always pays his pound.'

Mr Smee is ninety-three
But vibrant and alive,
He's never late, unlike his mate
Who died in sixty-five.
He plays the bongos badly
At a quite frenetic rate,
It lasts for several minutes
We just have to sit and wait.
Mrs Leith says through her teeth
'I cannot take much more!
If left to me, then Mr Smee
Would not reach ninety-four.'

The sisters Verne are very stern
They always think the same,
They tell us Joyce is vulgar,

And Picasso is a shame.
Wordsworth was a pantheist
And Lawrence was depraved,
Muggeridge might be all right,
But was he really saved?
C.S. Lewis wasn't quite
A fundamentalist,
And Dylan Thomas? Hopeless,
He was permanently paralytic.

Last week the members all agreed
That we should make a start,
On planning some more public way
To share abroad our art.
And so the works of Leith and Blair
And Grange and Voke and me,
Will grace the public library
For all the world to see.
What greater satisfaction
Than to help the unsaved find,
A glimpse, through our creations,
Of the *great* creator's mind?

Who Am I?
The Sensitivity of Sid

Names are very important.

I know a man who refuses to be introduced to strangers by his Christian name. He believes that shallow intimacy is achieved far too easily and cheaply nowadays, and that the casual exchange of forenames is often the first step in this unwelcome process. Similarly, he insists that his nephews and nieces address him as 'Uncle', rather than following the modern fashion of using his first name only.

He sees his name as a personal possession, something he values and shares with those who are close to him.

I am certainly very aware of my name, but, far

from valuing it, I have always felt uncomfortable about it. I very nearly hated it while I was at school. 'Adrian Plass' – I thought it sounded like a mouthful of plumbing tools. Most of all, I hated it when other boys took the mickey out of my name. It seemed a very specific, personal attack, not only on me, but, in a vague sort of way, on my family. How silly that sounds, but it really did make me very unhappy and angry – I expect that's why they did it.

Several years later I inadvertently upset someone very much because of a mistake I made in connection with his name.

It was Christmas, and during my vacation from College I was, for the second year running, contracted to work for the Post Office in Bromley during their busy period. I was looking forward to it. The previous year had been very enjoyable. Contrary to my own expectations I found it quite exhilarating to get up in the early hours, and ride my rickety old bike down to the sorting office in the dark. There were quite a lot of other students milling around when I arrived each morning. It was a pleasant atmosphere.

This year, instead of being allocated a normal delivery round as I had been the previous Christmas, I was asked to join a full-time regular driver on one of the parcel rounds. After much delay and many cups of tea in the canteen I was collected by my new partner, and we set off in his van to begin work. He was a young man of few words and, unfortunately, neither he nor anyone else had told me what his name was. Being something of a chinless wonder at the time I lacked the courage to ask for this information, so I was greatly relieved when we returned to the floor of the sorting office an hour or two later, to find that the problem was solved for me. My colleague seemed to be immensely popular.

'Hi, Sid! . . . wotcha, Sid, mate! . . . look, it's Sid! . . . Sid's 'ere! . . . had a good morning, Sid? . . .'

Cries of greeting went up from all sides. Everyone appeared to know and like my colleague. I couldn't quite see why. His response to all this warmth was ungracious, to say the least. He barely acknowledged the smiling welcome of his friends. Still, I reflected, at least I knew his name now. He was called Sid.

For the remainder of that working day I confidently addressed my workmate accordingly.

'Ill take this one, shall I, Sid? . . . cor, this is a heavy one, Sid! . . . Nearly time for tea, eh, Sid? . . .'

He was no more responsive to me than he had been to all those nice friends of his. In fact, if anything, he was getting grumpier and grumpier as the day wore on, until by the time we arrived back at the depot for the last time his expression was little short of thunderous. As he marched off towards the locker-room with a final grunt of farewell, I called out with unabated cheeriness:

'Cheers! See you tomorrow, Sid!'

The chorus of laughter from a nearby group of postmen that greeted this innocent cry was quite inexplicable to me. Sid stopped in his tracks, turned round and walked back towards me, his lips pressed angrily together, his cheeks flaming.

'My name's not Sid!' he hissed, his mouth about an inch from my ear.

'Not Sid?' I repeated, completely bewildered. 'But if you're not called Sid, why does everyone call you . . .'?'

'Because,' he interrupted, 'I drove into one of the brick gateposts last week and knocked it down. . . .'

'But what's that got to do with . . .?'

'And there's a demolition firm in Bromley called Sid Bishop Limited. That's why they call

221

me Sid. But my name's not SID!!'

'Oh.'

If I hadn't been quite so naïve I suppose I would have sensed what was going on much earlier. Poor Sid – I mean, poor . . . actually I never did find out what his real name was.

It was during that same holiday period that a grizzled old postman greeted me with the words: 'Hello, John!'

For some reason I had never encountered the name 'John' used as a generic term meaning 'mate' or 'friend'. My reply must have utterly confused the poor man.

'I think you've got it a bit wrong', I bleated, in my high-pitched, middle-class way. 'You must be thinking that I'm my brother John. I'm not John, I'm Adrian, but we are rather alike, so. . . .'

'Eh?' he said.

Nowadays, I don't really get very bothered about my own name but I am very conscious of the labels that people might attach to me. I seem to recall reading somewhere that Marx once said, 'I am not a Marxist'. I don't know if Jesus would say, 'I am not a Christian' if he returned in the flesh today, but one wonders. There are so many negative connotations attached to the 'religious' terms that we use all the time.

It intrigues me to think that there are many, many people outside organised religion, who would never come within the measuring scope of polls that set out to assess numbers of church-goers, but who would say they were Christians if the word had not become so devalued.

As for myself, I can't help being aware of the 'cringe factor' but I am very happy to be labelled as a follower of Jesus, albeit a stumbling one.

In fact, I'm more than happy, I'm genuinely proud to be associated with the name above all names.

If I belonged to a 'Believers Anonymous' group, I would stand up at the beginning of each meeting and say, 'My name is Adrian, and I'm a Christian'.

When Disaster Struck

But, what kind of Christian am I?

When things are easy, and the pressure of work has lifted temporarily, and I'm leaning back in my favourite armchair, and there are no emergencies, and the queue of worries has gone for lunch, and I *have* had a quiet time, and I've done the three vital things that I was supposed to do before my wife got back, and I haven't had a letter telling me that I write evil books, and I don't feel tired, and I've paid all the bills, and the dog has been walked, and it isn't what the British call a 'Glorious Day', and I haven't just realised that I've been booked to speak in Sunderland, Dudley and Tunbridge Wells on the same evening by three lots of people who've all been led by the Lord to ask me, and childhood spectres have taken a day off from haunting me, and I don't have indigestion, and every one of my four children is in a reasonably balanced state, and I'm not six months behind with unanswered post, and there isn't an ominous little knocking sound in the engine of my – alleged – car, and I'm not covered in Tipp-Ex from a squeeze bottle that didn't work and then suddenly did, and I'm feeling reasonably confident that God likes me, and I'm pretty sure that I like him – then, when all these conditions are fulfilled, I call myself a 'Jesus-loving relativist'.

It sounds quite impressive, doesn't it? All it means is that I am unswerving and uncompromising in my attitude to Jesus, but that my expression of this personal association is related to the needs, personalities and circumstances of the individual people I encounter.

This may seem naïvely obvious, but, strictly applied, such a philosophy can take one along strange uncharted paths that do not appear on many of the rather small-scale theological or doctrinal maps. I'm not talking about heresies, but the infinitely varied ways in which God works with people on a day-to-day basis. The gospel accounts of Jesus' ministry are very large-scale maps, little unexpected paths and by-ways in addition to the broad main roads of orthodoxy.

That's the sort of Christian I am when life is rolling along smoothly. I can (and do) talk and write about it a lot. It's easy to do that when things are going well.

Most of the time, though, like nearly everybody else that I know, my Christian faith is a tangle of joys and despairs, faith and doubt, certainty and unsureness, and all the other pairs of opposites that writers use to fill up space. I write and talk a lot about this muddled middle-path as well. It isn't quite so easy, but it is probably much more useful. Most of us know more about survival than victory.

What happens when disaster strikes? What sort of Christian am I when darkness and danger remove all my props and leave me helpless? What remains of the words and the ideas and the comfortable theorising when death stares me in the face?

In the summer of 1990 I had a chance to find out.

For our annual holiday that year we decided to take the car over to Denmark from Harwich on an extremely comfortable Scandinavian ferry. After a twenty-four hour journey we disembarked at the port of Esbjerg and drove north for a hundred miles or so to the little village of Stenvad in the Jurs peninsula, where our rented cottage awaited us.

Denmark was a land of rolling yellow corn-fields, green forest, enamel-blue skies and an unusually sparkling quality in the light. We were due to be there for a week before driving down through Germany to Holland, where I was to speak at the Flevo Festival for a day or two. On the third day of our Danish week we decided to visit a nearby theme park, known as Jurs Summerland.

We paid our entrance fees, parked the car, then explored the park, Bridget and I watching the children as they tried out the very large selection of rides and activities.

Halfway through the afternoon Bridget drifted off with Matthew, the eldest, while I queued with Joseph, David and Katy (eleven, ten and three at that time) to have a ride on the little circular boats that floated down an artificial river at quite considerable speed.

Hoping to balance our small craft, I sat the three children on one side and myself on the other. It still 'dipped' a little on my side, but it was reasonably trim. Away we went, our small craft spinning slowly round as it was swept along by the current.

Somehow, perhaps because safety regulations are quite rigidly enforced in most similar situations in this country, one expects that nothing much can go wrong. This time, everything went wrong.

As the boat reached a point where the river was straddled by a little brick bridge, the level of the water dropped abruptly and its speed increased slightly. Without warning the boat overturned completely, tipping all of us into the river and trapping me on my back under the water.

Lying there, my belt snagged by some projection on the riverbed, the weight of the upturned boat pressing like a coffin full of rocks on my chest, the following thoughts went through my mind.

First, quite incredibly, I said to myself: 'If I get out of this alive, it'll make a jolly good article or broadcast.' I suppose that just shows how pathetically desperate we writers are to find new material.

Secondly, eclipsing that ridiculous initial reaction, came blind panic. How was I, a non-swimmer, going to free myself to look for Katy? Where *was* Katy? Had she hit her head? Was she drowning? Was she already dead? What about the boys? Where were they? They were strong swimmers, but . . . .

Suddenly, the sheer horror of the situation screamed through my brain in the darkness. Like a small child I cried out in my mind to the only person who could help me.

'God, get me out of this . . . river!!'

With a final desperate heave I pushed the boat off my chest, thereby dislodging the other end of the craft, which was resting on the shelf in the riverbank that had caused the problem in the first place.

Standing up and gasping for breath, I pushed the wet hair away from my eyes and looked around. The two boys were swimming around unscathed, wild-eyed but safe. Katy had completely disappeared. Joe and David adore their little sister. The tearful panic in their voices as they called out to me was a perfect echo of the emotion that paralysed me for a moment as I tried to think what to do next. Where, oh where, was Katy?

I started to feel around under the water, hoping and dreading that I would find her there somewhere. In the space of a few seconds I saw the hypothetical events of the following few days as vividly as if they had already happened: the abrupt termination of our holiday: the miserable

return to England: telling everybody: the funeral
. . . .

'She's under the boat, Dad! She's under the boat!'

The boys had swum down to where the still upside-down boat was lodged against the bank. David could hear Katy calling me from inside the air-pocket between the surface of the water and the bottom of the inverted craft.

Frantically, I made my way down to where the boys were vainly battling to free their sister. Putting both hands under the rim of the boat I heaved with all my strength, but my efforts were useless. It wouldn't budge. Almost whimpering with frustration I threw out another silent prayer, gritted my teeth and heaved again. The boat lifted and turned in a cloud of spray as I fell back into the water again. Struggling back onto my feet, the first thing I saw was my daughter bobbing gently up and down in the water a few yards away. Her hair was hardly wet, and her expression was remarkably untroubled.

'Hello, Daddy,' she said, as Joe pushed and pulled her up on to the bank. 'I knew I'd be all right, 'cos you were here.'

When I finally held Katy I nearly squeezed her to death. It had, without any doubt, been the most alarming experience of my life.

On the positive side, though, it had answered my question about what kind of Christian I would be when disaster threatened, and ritual, churchmanship, theology and all the man-made paraphernalia of religion were irrelevant. The answer was that I became a frightened child who called out, with primitive trust, to the only person who could possibly help.

We cannot avoid physical danger, illness and other problems, Jesus made that quite clear. I thank God that Katy is still with us; other parents (Christians included) have not been so fortunate, and that is a dark mystery that I don't pretend to understand. But, whether or not disaster strikes in this world, I could ask for nothing more than to be the kind of Christian who says to God, rather as Katy optimistically said to me: 'I knew I'd be all right, because you were here.'

Falling Off

I fall off the bouncy castle from time to time –
don't you? Also, like the pathetic prodigal son
that I am, I take an occasional day excursion back
to the 'pigs', drawn like an insect to the sticky-
sweetness of sin. But when the feverish glow of
self-indulgence has paled I feel dreadful. I used
to feel frightened as well. Jesus' words about the
unworthiness of people who put their hands to
the plough and then turn back are rather alarming when you look around and see the haphazard
and incomplete state of your own particular field.

But, returning from the world of pigs, insects
and ploughs to our original bouncy castle image –
why *would* I want to get off? Why exchange a

clearer view of heaven for the stolid pseudo-realism of an earthly perspective? Am I mad?

No; I am unfit.

Why would I not last too long on a real bouncy castle? First, because I am overweight and unused to exercise. I would be puffing and blowing like a walrus after five minutes. The spiritual daily work-out requires a régime of regular prayer press-ups, and biblical bull-working, although the strictness of the discipline involved is really only intended as a framework within which I can be as daft as a brush with God – like a child on a bouncy castle in fact.

Secondly, my sense of balance is faulty. After bouncing around for a while I start to get dizzy and lose my footing. The rules for staying upright in the Kingdom of Heaven are quite different from the ones we're used to. It can be quite a relief to plant your feet on familiar and apparently solid ground. It takes lots of practice, and not a little courage, to accept a completely different basis for being.

Thirdly, and this is one we don't hear very much about, I get bored after a while. Obsessional by nature, I am quite likely to do nothing but castle-bouncing once I'm fit enough, and I've learned to keep my footing. The analogy becomes a little er . . . deflated at this point, but it is undoubtedly a fact that many people fall away from faith after obsessionally enthusiastic involvement in one narrow aspect of church life or theology, usually because a particular need has not been met at a particular time. The fall can be tragically hard. In fact, of course, God is in all places and activities that can benefit from his presence; light and pleasant or dark and desperate. He is there, inviting us to give our hands for his use in an enormous variety of ways, some of which offer a chance of real adventure. It is the limits I draw around myself and God that can sometimes result in boredom.

Does God condemn us when we fail in these ways? If he does, then I was condemned a long time ago, and many times since (if that makes any sense).

No, I don't believe that God condemns his bouncy-castle children. I do believe he corrects, coaxes and disciplines us just as an earthly father would, and that his ultimate aim for each of us is total purity of motivation, behaviour and perspective. The chances of achieving such perfection on this side of heaven may be nil, but if things do go wrong we know that Jesus will plead for us more eloquently than we ever could. We need to go on believing that – like children.

So keep on bouncing!

See you on the bouncy castle.

Fount Paperbacks

Fount is one of the leading paperback publishers of religious books and below are some of its recent titles.

- ☐ PAUL THE INTERPRETER George Appleton £2.95
- ☐ ACTING AS FRIENDS Michael De-la-Noy £4.50
- ☐ THE BURNING BUSH John Drury £2.99
- ☐ A KEY TO THE OLD TESTAMENT
  David Edwards £3.50
- ☐ THE CRY OF THE SPIRIT Tatiana Goricheva £3.99
- ☐ CROSSFIRE Richard Holloway £3.50
- ☐ CREATION Martin Israel £2.99
- ☐ BEING IN LOVE William Johnston £3.50
- ☐ THE MASS J. M. Lustiger £2.99
- ☐ CALLED TO HOLINESS Ralph Martin £2.95
- ☐ THE HIDDEN JOURNEY Melvyn Matthews £3.50
- ☐ REFLECTIONS ON MY WORK Thomas Merton £3.99
- ☐ DEATH BE NOT PROUD Peter Mullen £2.99
- ☐ SCRIPTURE PROMISES Carmen Rojas £3.50
- ☐ LIGHT AND LIFE Grazyna Sikorska £2.95
- ☐ EASTER GARDEN Nicola Slee £3.95
- ☐ CHRISTMAS – AND ALWAYS Rita Snowden £2.99
- ☐ CELEBRATION Margaret Spufford £2.95

All Fount Paperbacks are available at your bookshop or newsagent, or they can be ordered by post from Fount Paperbacks, Cash Sales Department, G.P.O. Box 29, Douglas, Isle of Man. Please send purchase price plus 22p per book, maximum postage £3. Customers outside the UK send purchase price, plus 22p per book. Cheque, postal order or money order. No currency.

NAME (Block letters) _____

ADDRESS_____

_____

_____